ORIGAMI
CARD CRAFT
30 CLEVER CARDS and ENVELOPES to FOLD

KAREN ELAINE THOMAS

POTTER
CRAFT

NEW YORK

THIS BOOK IS DEDICATED to my parents, for giving me an endless supply of crayons and paper and for encouraging me to pursue a career as an artist, and to my children, Eric, Sarah, and Lauren, who inspired me to be playful with paper.

Contents

Introduction

A handmade card will always delight its recipient more than a store-bought one.

It's simple: The energy and thought that go into a personal, cleverly folded card show your friend or family member how much you care.

I discovered this many years ago while working in an art supply store in Santa Barbara, California. I was intrigued by all the beautiful textures, colors, and patterns available in the paper department, and my passion for paper and origami began. I found handmade greeting cards inspired by origami to be the perfect craft to make for friends, since they allowed me to express my creativity with very little cost and in very little time.

Completely enthralled by the works of talented origami designers from all over the world, I quickly became an origami enthusiast. I experimented with traditional folds and incorporated traditional shapes into my cards. I started to design my own simple geometric shapes to add dimension to my cards, and I applied shimmering paints and other embellishments. I found card making to be a less intimidating way to experiment with the vast world of art supplies and the art of paper folding than doing larger projects like painting and collage. But most of all, I loved incorporating origami into my cards, creating a unique statement, and expressing my creativity while connecting with the card's recipient.

In the pages that follow, you will find the directions and inspiration for a variety of folded greeting cards for any occasion. You will learn the basics of origami folding so that you can play with the shapes and forms and invent your own creative cards, just as I did. Find colors and patterns that suit your own unique style. But most of all, have fun making cards for your friends and family.

Happy folding!
KAREN ELAINE

Origami Basics

Paper, Tools, and Supplies

Having the proper tools and materials will open up a world of playful, creative expression. Many of the supplies needed for these cards may already be in your home—in your kitchen, garage, or sewing room. Hardware, craft, and art supply stores have a huge selection of products available, but card making does not have to be expensive. Save wrapping paper, grocery bags, and anything else that might look good on a card. Just recently, while hiking through a canyon not far from my home, I found several beautifully shaped oak leaves that had just fallen from the tree. I took some of the best-looking ones because I knew that someday I would find a use for them in one of my projects.

Here is a list of the basic tools you will need for the cards in this book:

PAPER

Get creative: You can use wrapping paper, origami paper, decorative paper, paper bags, and even office paper. When selecting paper, fold a corner back and forth to make sure the folds don't crack.

CUTTING SUPPLIES

A cutting surface, such as a self-healing cutting mat, a cutting knife, such as an X-Acto® knife, and a metal-edged ruler are needed to cut the papers. A paper cutter is very handy but not absolutely necessary.

BLANK GREETING CARDS, 5" X 7" (12.5CM X 18CM) WHEN CLOSED

These can be purchased at art supply and craft stores as well as office supply stores. My favorite blank greeting card is the Strathmore Watercolor Card because it is heavier than most blank cards and can be painted. Blank greeting cards come in a variety of colors and almost always come with matching envelopes.

GREETING CARD STOCK

Greeting card stock is a heavyweight paper that is great for backing your folded elements and adding to the design of your card. Purchase various colors and simple patterns to have on hand when you are making cards.

ORIGAMI PAPER

Origami paper comes in all kinds of colors, textures, and patterns, and is always perfectly square. It is usually lightweight, which makes it easier to fold into more complex designs.

SCRAPBOOK PAPER

Scrapbook paper is heavier in weight than origami paper and comes in an amazing variety of patterns, solids, and double-sided coordinates.

Some scrapbook papers come in 6" (15cm) and 12" (30.5cm) squares, which are perfect for paper folding! Make extra sure the paper you choose can be folded without cracking; not all scrapbook papers are suitable for folding for this reason.

DECORATIVE PAPERS

This could include just about any paper available. There are beautiful patterned, textured, and solid papers from Japan, India, France, and Thailand, which you can find at art supply and craft stores as well as on the Internet. Some come in full-sized (parent) sheets, which can be quite large, and others come in packages or as single sheets in assorted standard sizes (such as 8½" x 11" [21.5cm x 28cm], 12" x 12" (30.5cm x 30.5cm], or A4). Most decorative papers can be folded or used as a background for your cards.

GLUES AND ADHESIVES

I use a glue stick for light applications and PVA (polyvinyl acetate, or bookbinder's glue) or white glue, such as Elmer's, for a stronger bond. Various widths of high-tack double-sided tape, also known as red liner tape, are also indispensable when attaching ribbon or embellishments.

GLUE APPLICATOR

A stiff brush, a piece of cardboard, or an old credit card can be used to spread glue evenly. Adhesive applicator designed for the purpose, such as a Xyron, are also very helpful when making cards. The other advantage to an applicator is that it keeps glue off your hands!

STAMP PADS, RUBBER STAMPS, AND ACRYLIC PAINTS

Having a supply of decorating supplies to enhance your cards will make them stand out even more.

EMBELLISHMENTS

Ribbon, thread, brads, paper cords, tassels and other fun embellishments will add the finishing touch to your creations. The Pinwheel card (page 38) calls for a pronged metal brad or button brad, also known as a paper fastener. These are available at craft or office supply stores. The Folded Frame card (page 46) is decorated with a tassel, available at craft supply stores.

SMALL ⅛" (3MM) ROUND HOLE PUNCH

You will need a punch to make small holes for stitching. Many paper hole punches are available and range from inexpensive to pricey. My favorite punch is the Japanese screw punch. It goes through several sheets of paper and thick cardboard, allows you to place the hole anywhere, and has different tip sizes for versatility. Before I discovered the screw punch, I used a hammer and assorted nail sizes to make holes.

BONE FOLDER

I find bone folders perfect for making very clean creases. You can also use one to score your cards to make folding the card stock much easier and the result more professional. Bone folders can be made of bone, wood, or plastic material.

PAINTS AND INKS TO DECORATE PLAIN PAPER

As a child, I found much joy in gliding my fingertips through a gooey mixture of poster paint on slick paper to make my own wonderful patterns and designs. Finger painting is one playful way to decorate plain papers, but there are several techniques based on the art of faux finishing that will give even your plainest papers their own distinctive look. Sponge or brush acrylic paint onto your paper for a stippled effect, or crinkle up a plastic bag, dip it into paint, and dab it onto the paper for a marbled look. Use paint that will not be tacky when it dries, such as Golden Artist Colors or Jacquard Lumiere acrylics. Paints specifically designed for paper are also available at major craft stores. Before you start making cards, you may want to have a "paper play day" to make an assortment of exciting and unusual decorative papers so that you will have several colors and patterns to choose from.

Creating a work space

As important as it is to have the right tools, papers, and embellishments on hand, creating a space for them is equally important. Make sure your supplies are organized in a way that makes them easily accessible, so that when you feel the urge to create (and that can happen at any time), you will have them at your fingertips. I use clear plastic boxes to store my blank cards, pens, tapes, and other supplies so that I can easily find what I want when I need it. I organize my papers into color groups, such as blues, golds, reds, and patterns, in separate clear, flat containers. Finally, find a large, flat surface, such as a kitchen table, to use as a workspace when creating your cards.

Folding 101

I started folding paper in earnest several years ago when I discovered the works of master origami artists. The designs fascinated me, and I liked the idea that the boxes were functional as well as beautiful. The projects were simple, but I found many of them difficult to construct because I had not yet mastered the basic symbols common to all origami diagrams.

Below is a list of the basic symbols and folds that you will find in the diagrams for the cards in this book. Once you familiarize yourself with the basic folding instructions found in traditional books and diagrams, you will be able to understand the patterns in this book and fold them precisely. Origami is a universal language, so once you learn it, you can read books printed in any language, even Japanese or Russian.

BASIC FOLDS

 An even dotted line tells you to **valley fold**.

 The paper edges go up and the fold goes down, like a valley between two slopes.

 A dot-dash line tells you to **mountain fold**.

The paper edges go down and the fold comes up like the peak of a mountain.

 A solid line shows that a fold has already been made; such lines are often used as landmarks to fold to.

For a **cupboard fold**, which opens and closes like a cupboard door, make two folds to a center crease line.

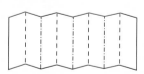 For an **accordion fold**, alternate equally spaced mountain and valley folds to create an accordion, which is also known as a fan fold.

BASIC ARROWS

 The single-line arrow tells you to fold in the direction of the arrow and then move on to the next step.

 The double-line arrow tells you to fold in the direction of the arrow and unfold before going to the next step.

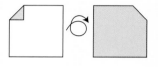 The looped arrow tells you to turn the paper over and work on the other side.

Not all diagrams are created equal. Some may be more difficult to follow than others, but don't be discouraged. After all, it's only paper; it's usually inexpensive. As you progress in folding, you'll challenge yourself with more complex folds and amaze yourself and your friends. It's a wonderful feeling to turn something as simple as a sheet of paper into a delightful creation that brings joy to everyone who receives it.

Now, start gathering your supplies and papers and have some fun making cool, creative cards!

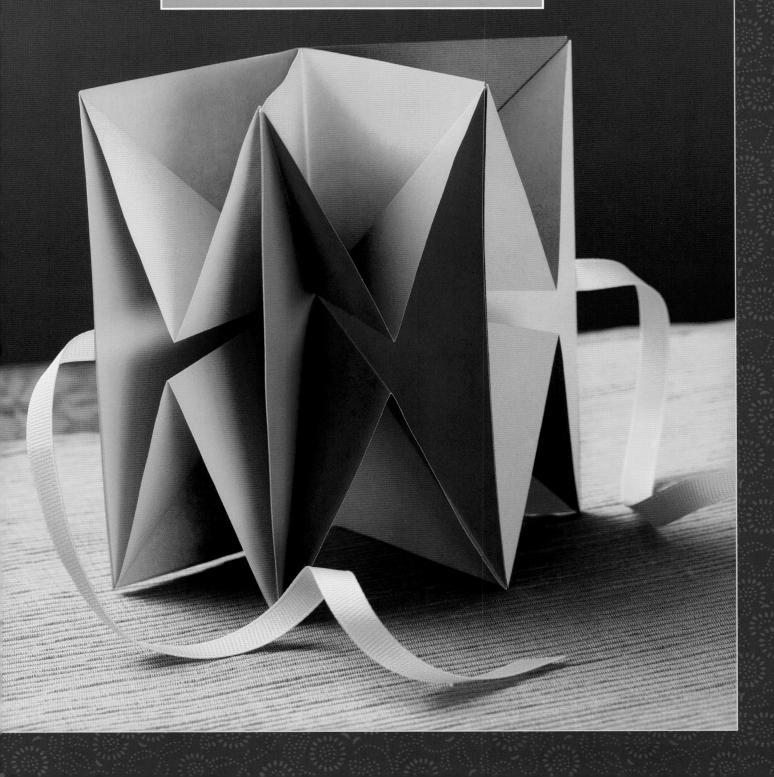

CARDS

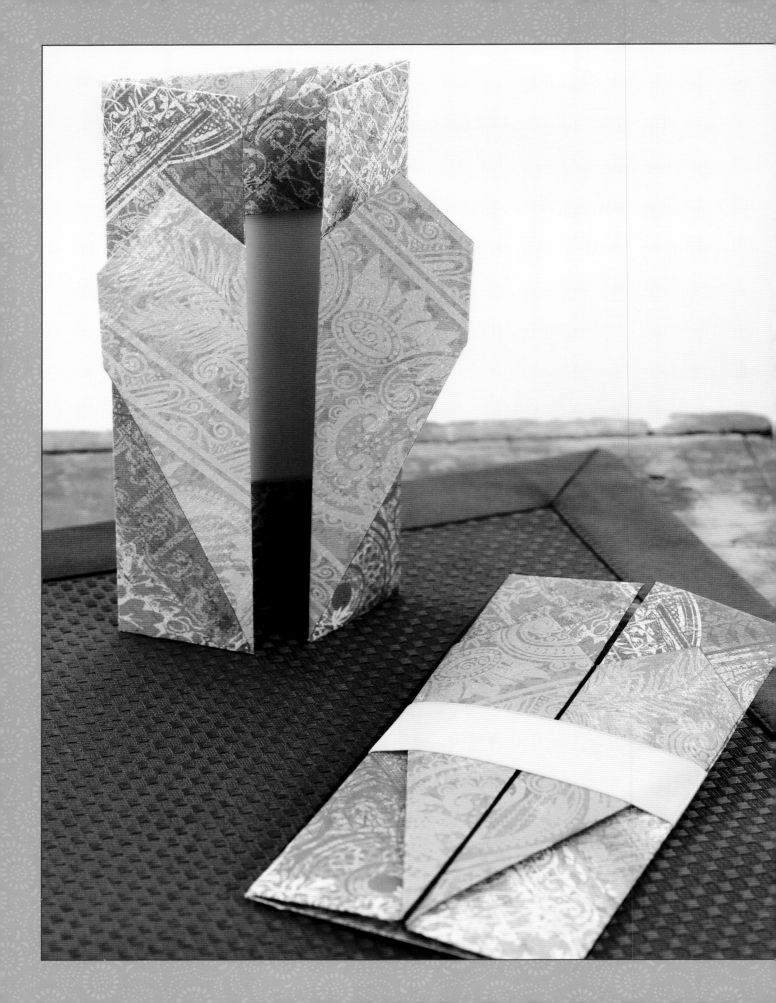

Fold-Out Heart

The heart has long been a symbol of love and compassion, and this very easy-to-fold card will warm the heart of the receiver. It can be sent as a valentine or wedding invitation, or used as a picture frame. Since this is an odd-sized card, you will need to create a matching envelope (see instructions on page 108).

MATERIALS

1 sheet double-sided medium-weight scrapbook paper cut to 10" (25.5cm) square

Scissors

Glue stick

1"- (2.5cm-) wide ribbon

Double-sided tape

Card stock cut 3¼" x 6¾" (8cm x 17cm)

FOR ENVELOPE:

1 sheet coordinating paper cut to 14½" x 7" (37cm x 18cm)

FINISHED SIZE

3½" x 7" (9cm x 18cm)

FOLD THE CARD

 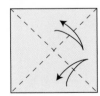

Place the double-sided paper with the side for the heart facing up. Valley fold the sheet of paper in half in both diagonal directions and then unfold.

Valley fold all 4 corners to meet in the center.

Valley fold the top and bottom corners so the points touch the outer edge.

11

4

5

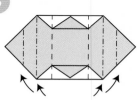

6

With the points still folded, valley fold the left and right sides to meet in the center.

Open out the sides just folded completely, so the points face left and right.

Make the outer 2 folds on each pointed flap into mountain creases. Refold along new creases back toward the center.

10

11

12

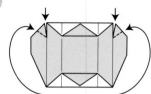

Repeat steps 8 and 9 for the left side.

Your paper should have two angled flaps on a cupboard fold.

Open out the right and left sides as shown in the diagram and cut a slit about 1⅝" (4cm) long at the top of the outermost crease on each side. Mountain fold the little cut sections in so the outside edges line up. Turn the paper over and glue down the loose folds of the heart shape. Turn the paper over again.

DECORATE THE CARD AND MAKE AN ENVELOPE

1 Wrap a piece of 1"- (2.5cm-) wide ribbon around the card and glue or tape the ends together to secure, but do not glue the ribbon to the card, as it needs to easily slide on and off the card.

2 Fold the sheet of coordinating paper to fit exactly around the card according to the instructions for the Simple Envelope on page 108.

7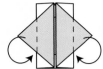

Mountain fold the outer flaps just underneath themselves (but not all the way around the card).

8

Valley fold the right top layer to the left as if turning the page of a book.

9

Valley fold the bottom corner of the top layer over to the right to meet the crease line, then mountain fold the top layer back to the right.

13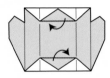

Mountain fold the top and bottom points underneath.

14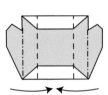

Fold the sides back to the center along the existing creases.

tip: To make the heart stand out even more, paint the heart edges with a contrasting color of acrylic paint, line them with a metallic paint marker, or run a metallic stamp pad edge along them.

Fortune Teller

The fold that inspired this card is also known as the salt cellar. The fortune teller uses a traditional origami fold that was originally designed in Japan to hold spices. Today, it is used to play a game great for children's parties and school functions but also enjoyed by adults. This interactive card can be made for any occasion, and you can fold a matching envelope (see instructions for making the Simple Envelope on page 108, using a 7″ x 12″ [18cm x 30.5cm] piece of paper).

I bought my fortune cookies at a local Asian market and enjoyed eating every one of them! You can also write your own fortunes and print them on an inkjet printer or copy machine.

MATERIALS

1 sheet double-sided medium-weight printed paper cut to 11″ (28cm) square

4 large letters of the alphabet, such as A–D, and 8 medium sized numbers, such as 1–8, from your printer, rubber stamps, or letters cut from a magazine

Glue stick

8 Fortune cookie fortunes

FINISHED SIZE

3″ x 6″ (7.5cm x 15cm) when folded in half

CARD ASSEMBLY

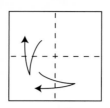

If your paper is colored on only one side, start with the colored side down. Fold the paper in half and unfold in both directions.

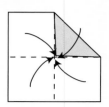

Fold all corners to the center.

Valley fold in half.

Insert your fingers into all 4 pockets to open.

DECORATE THE CARD

Glue the large letters on the four outer squares while the fortune teller is still folded.

Open the card at the center horizontal fold and glue the numbers on each triangle area. You should have 8 shapes on which to glue the numbers.

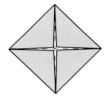

 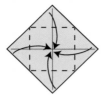

You should have folded lines that cross at the center of the paper. Turn the paper over.

Valley fold all 4 corners to meet in the center.

how to play:

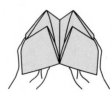

1. Slide your thumbs and fingers under the 4 exterior flaps.

2. Rotate your hands inward, bringing your thumbs and index fingers together. The fortune teller should expand. The numbered triangles will disappear inside, like the middle of a flower when the petals close.

3. Pick a letter and open the fortune teller forward and back and side-to-side for each letter. For instance, if you pick the letter C, open and close 3 times leaving the inside open to pick a number (letters correspond to numbers based on alphabetical sequence).

4. Pick a number from the inside and open and close as many times as the number. For instance, if you pick the number 8, open and close it 8 times.

5. Pick another number inside and lift the flap the number is printed on to reveal your fortune!

 3

Open up the 4 pointed flaps and glue the fortunes on the outer edge of each triangular area, keeping the fortune inside the crease lines. Close the card back up.

Little Pocket

For this card, a long strip of paper is folded to create a pocket in which you can insert a cute little pamphlet greeting. Write on or decorate the plain side of the strip before folding to reveal a special message when the card is unfolded. This card can be used for table settings at weddings or special occasions, and it makes a great gift card.

MATERIALS

1 sheet medium-weight decorative paper cut to 3" x 15" (7.5cm x 38cm)

1 sheet card stock cut to 2¾" x 5½" (7cm x 14cm)

1 sheet paper cut to 2⅝" x 4⅜" (6.7cm x 11.1cm)

⅛" (3mm) hole punch

Decorative thread and needle

Double-sided tape

¼"- (6mm-) wide coordinating ribbon

Cutting knife

Metal straightedge

1 sheet medium-weight decorative paper cut to 2¾" x 5½" (7cm x 14cm)

FINISHED SIZE

Approximately 3¹⁄₁₆" x 3¹⁄₁₆" (7.8cm x 7.8cm)

FOLD THE CARD

 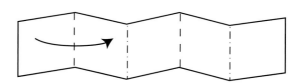

Write or stamp a message on the wrong side of the long strip of decorative paper. Then accordion fold the strip into 5 square sections and unfold.

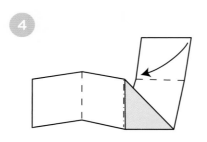

Valley fold the top square in half diagonally to meet the first crease.

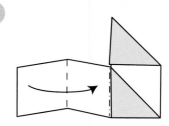

Valley fold the left-most square on the crease.

MAKE THE BOOKLET

Hold the small sheet of card stock and 2⅝" x 4⅜" (6.7cm x 11.1cm) paper together and fold in half to make a little booklet.

Punch 3 small holes on the crease line about 1" (2.5cm) apart.

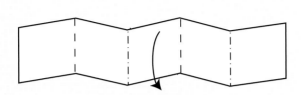

Valley fold the strip diagonally in the middle section.

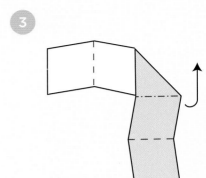

Mountain fold the strip under along the first crease below the diagonal fold.

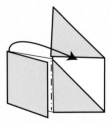

Mountain fold the sections just folded under the triangle to the right.

Valley fold the remaining triangular panel down and tuck it into the triangular pocket.

Tuck the remaining triangle into the pocket.

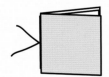

With the outside facing up and using a needle and thread, pass the thread down through the center hole, then go up through one of the other holes and out the top, crossing over the center hole and back down through the remaining hole. Bring the needle back up through the center hole and tie the ends to secure.

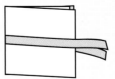

With the booklet card open and with the cover facing up, apply a ¼"- (6mm-) wide strip of double-sided tape lengthwise across the middle of the outside of the book. Apply the ribbon to the tape and trim the ends to the desired length.

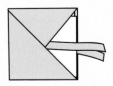

The booklet will slide nicely under the two triangle flaps into the card pocket.

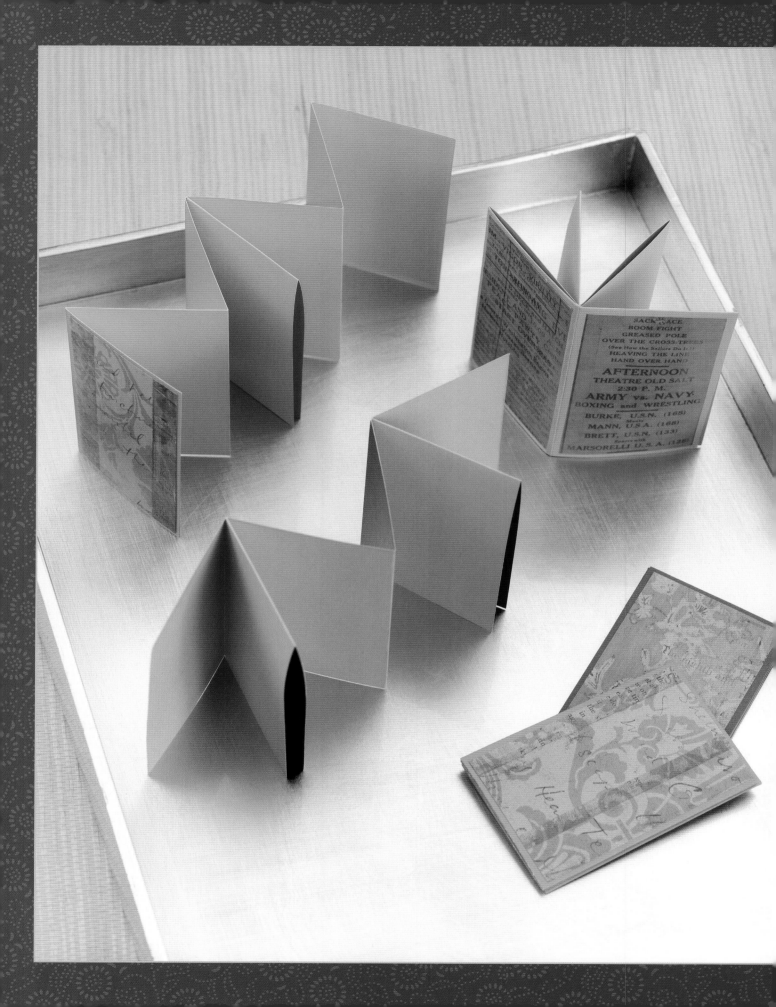

Cut and Fold

These simple one-sheet folded cards open up like little books. You can display children's art, photos, or thoughts and decorate the front and back covers for an unusual greeting card that your recipient will cherish. The simple folding directions apply to all three cards, but the cutting patterns are different. Be sure your folds and cuts are accurate. Experiment with different sizes of paper and new folds for more interesting variations.

MATERIALS

1 sheet 8½" x 11" (21.5cm x 28cm) medium-weight (24-lb) colored office paper

Cutting knife or scissors

Metal straightedge

FOR FRONT AND BACK COVERS:

2 sheets of decorative paper or card stock cut to approximately 2½" x 4" (6.5cm x 10cm)

FINISHED SIZE

2¾" x 4¼" (7cm x 11cm)

VARIATION I

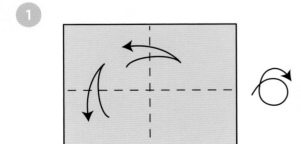

Orient the paper landscape style. Fold the paper in half and unfold in both directions. Turn over.

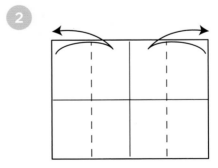

Cupboard fold the outermost edges to the center fold, and unfold to create 8 equal sections.

3

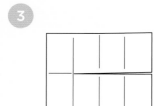

Using scissors or a ruler and straightedge, carefully cut a slit along the center crease going through the right-most 3 sections only.

4

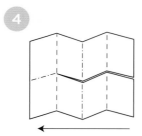

Fold the bottom right-most 3 sections along the existing creases, and then reverse the crease along the center crease and continue to fold the remaining 3 sections in an accordion style along the existing creases.

5

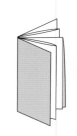

Your folded card will have a front and back cover, 8 facing pages, and a back cover, with a tent in the center of the pages. Glue the 2 pieces of decorative paper or card stock to the front and back covers to give strength to the card. Use the remaining pages for a special greeting.

4

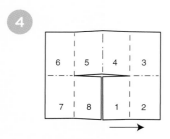

Starting at the first section on the right side of the slit, accordion fold along the existing valley crease and then mountain fold at the next section.

5

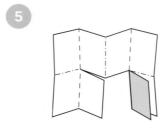

Valley fold the next section along the existing crease and mountain fold the next crease.

6

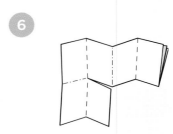

Continue folding along the existing creases counterclockwise until you reach the last section.

3

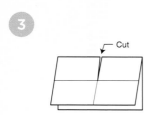

Fold the paper in half vertically and cut a slit from the folded edge at the center to the first inter-secting crease. Unfold the paper.

4

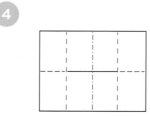

To make the folding easier, prepare to valley and mountain fold as shown in the diagram.

5

Mountain fold the paper in half lengthwise. The slit will be at the top.

VARIATION II

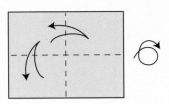 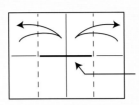 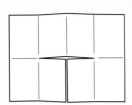

Orient the paper landscape style. Fold the paper in half lengthwise, unfold, and fold the paper in half in the other direction. Unfold and turn the paper over.

Valley fold the left and right edges to the center and unfold. Cut through the center lengthwise, leaving the right and left outer-most sections solid.

Cut through the bottom middle crease up to the first slit.

VARIATION III

 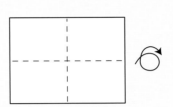 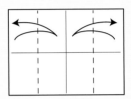

Your folded card will have a front and back cover, 8 facing pages, and a back cover, with 2 "tents" among the pages. Glue the 2 pieces of decorative paper or card stock to the front and back covers to give strength to the card. Use the remaining pages for a special greeting.

Orient the paper landscape style. Valley fold the paper in half horizontally and vertically. Unfold the paper and turn it over.

Cupboard fold the vertical edges to the center fold and unfold.

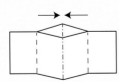 

While folded, push the sides together, forming a diamond from the slit, until the solid, uncut edges meet.

Collapse all pages together and crease so that all of the pages are evenly lined up. Your folded card will have a front and back cover, 8 facing pages, and a back cover, with 2 "tents" among the pages. Glue the 2 pieces of decorative paper or card stock to the front and back covers to give strength to the card. Use the remaining pages for a special greeting.

Love Knot

This elegant knot symbolizes long-lasting love or the ties among friends and family. The paper ribbon strip tucked into the knot represents unity. Choose colors that are special to you and the recipient, and write something about the colors inside the card to give your greeting a more personal character.

MATERIALS

2 sheets contrasting fibrous paper cut to 4" x 11" (10cm x 11cm) strips

Thin-bodied white glue

Glue applicator, such as an old credit card or a piece of cardboard

Cutting knife with metal straightedge or scissors

1 blank greeting card, 5" x 7" (12.5cm x 18cm) when closed

Coordinating decorative paper or card stock cut slightly smaller than the front of the greeting card

Double-sided tape

6" (15cm) length Mizuhiki paper cord ribbon or ¼"- (6mm-) wide ribbon

FINISHED SIZE

5" x 7" (12.5cm x 18cm) when closed

FOLD THE KNOT

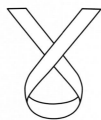

Valley fold the 2 strips in half lengthwise and fold the 2 outer-most edges to the center fold. Open the folds and apply a thin coat of glue to the entire surface facing up. Close the outermost folds back up. Each strip will now measure about 1" x 11" (2.5cm x 28cm). While the glue is still wet and the paper is pliable, form a large loop in the middle of one strip, with the ends of the strip pointing away from you.

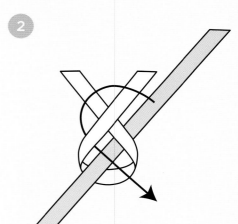

Introduce the second strip from the front. Bring it through and behind the first loop, then bring it forward and thread it through the lower part of the loop.

ASSEMBLE THE CARD

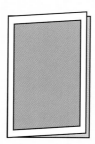

Glue the coordinating decorative card stock or paper to the front of the blank greeting card.

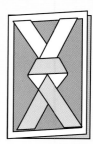

Apply double-sided tape to the back of the knot and stick it to the front of the card stock.

3

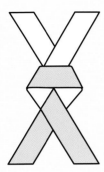

Gently pull the opposite ends of the paper strips at the same time to form the knot. Tighten the knot carefully, making sure the paper lies flat. The center of the knot will form a perfect hexagon when flattened. Let the glue in the knot dry thoroughly, and trim ends to the desired length with a cutting knife or scissors.

tip: The paper for this knot should be strong yet thin, such as Japanese or handmade fibrous papers.

3

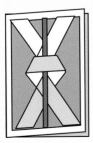

Run the piece of ribbon through the center of the knot for an added accent, and trim to desired length.

Secret Slipcase

Your friends will be amazed when they receive this functional and fun card, with its several small pockets in which to tuck notes, photos, greetings, or business cards. This card can be slipped into your purse for an easy way to show off your grandkids, favorite pet, or friends. Write a secret message in the little stitch-bound booklet, and slide it into one of the inside pockets. The folding is simple, but the result is dramatic.

MATERIALS

1 sheet decorative paper cut to
10″ x 13¾″ (25.5cm x 35cm)

Glue stick

14″ (35.5cm) length ⅛″– (3mm–)
wide decorative ribbon in a
coordinating color

1 sheet contrasting paper cut to
4″ x 5½″ (10cm x 14cm)

1 sheet card stock (for booklet) cut
to 5⅞″ x 3¹⁵⁄₁₆″ (14.9cm x 10cm)

1 sheet lightweight paper cut to
5¾″ x 3⅞″ (14.5cm x 9.8cm)

⅛″ (3mm) hole punch

Needle and thread

2 sheets card stock (to slip in
pockets) cut to 3″ x 3¹⁵⁄₁₆″
(7.5cm x 10cm)

FINISHED SIZE

Approximately 3⅜″ x 4⅛″
(8.6cm x 10.5cm)

FOLD THE SLIPCASE

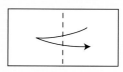

Start with the 10″ x 13¾″ (25.5cm x
35cm) sheet of decorative paper,
oriented landscape style with the
color you want on the outside
facing down. Valley fold in half
crosswise and then unfold.

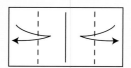

Cupboard fold the 2 sides to meet
the center crease. Unfold.

Mountain fold the top at the
folded corner edges and turn the
paper over.

Valley fold the bottom edge up to
meet the top edge. Tuck the
corners into the triangle-shaped
pockets.

FOLD THE INSIDE BOOKLET

Fold the booklet card stock and lightweight paper in half crosswise and
punch 3 small holes evenly spaced on the crease, approximately 1½″
(3.8cm) apart.

3

Valley fold the side edges to the nearest creases on the right and left sides. Crease well.

4

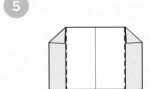

Valley fold the top corners at a 45-degree angle so the top edge aligns with the nearest crease (below the flaps)

5

Valley fold along the existing outermost creases on both sides

8

Fold in half from left to right to close the piece like a book.

9

Unfold the card back to step 7 and glue a piece of ribbon across the middle on the inside, leaving enough ribbon on each side to tie to secure the card closed. Close the card back up by tucking the corners back into the triangle pockets.

10

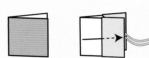

Fold the 4" x 5½" (10cm x 14cm) sheet in half crosswise and slip it into the front and back outer large pockets of the slipcase.

2

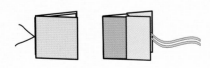

With the outside of the booklet facing up and using a needle and thread, pass the thread down through the center hole, then go up through one of the other holes and out the top, crossing over the center hole and back down through the remaining hole. Bring the needle back up through the center hole and tie the ends to secure.

tip: To make the case lay flat when closed, fold creases ⅛" (3mm) from each side of the center crease of the slip-case to create a ¼"- (6mm-) wide "spine." This is a great technique for thicker cards and booklets.

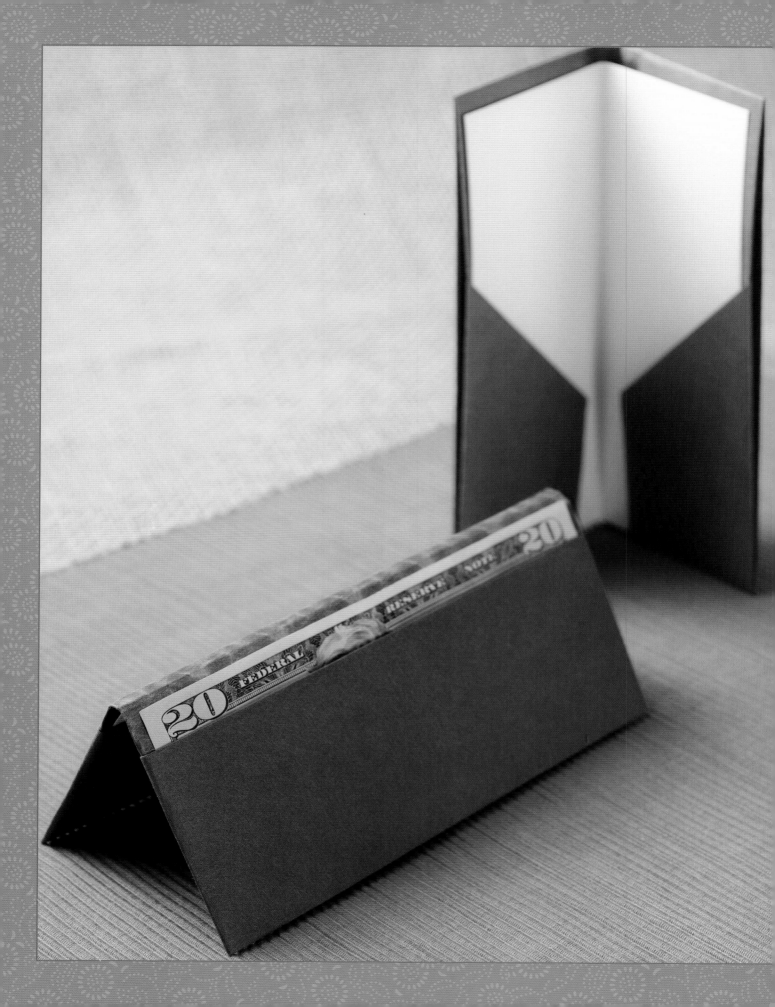

Money Holder

This clever little card can easily do double duty as a gift-money holder. Depending on the size paper you use, this fold can be applied to create a variety of practical paper purses or wallets. The kind of paper you use and whether or not it is printed on both sides will determine the holder's final look.

MATERIALS

1 sheet decorative paper cut to
12″ x 17″ (30.5cm x 43cm)

Greeting card stock cut to 5″ x 6″
(12.5cm x 15cm)

ALTERNATIVE PAPER SIZES

FOR PASSPORT CASE:

12″ x 16″ (30.5cm x 40.5cm)

FOR BUSINESS OR CREDIT
CARD CASE:

8½″ x 11″ (21.5cm x 28cm)

FOR POSTAGE STAMP CASE:

6″ x 6″ (15cm x 15cm)

FINISHED SIZE

6⅜″ x 3⅞″ (16.2cm x 9.8cm)

FOLD THE CARD

 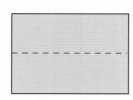

Place the paper landscape style on
a flat surface, colored or patterned
side up. Fold it in half lengthwise.

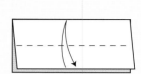

Valley fold the top layer to the top
edge. Crease well, then unfold.
Turn the paper over and repeat
on the other side.

 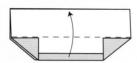

Valley fold each side on the
previously creased line. The edges
will no longer meet at the center
crease because of the ½″ (13mm)
hem on each side.

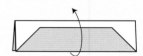

Open on the center crease and
turn the paper over so that all of
the folded edges are facing down.

 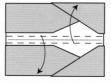

To make the card close flat, fold ⅛″
(3mm) from each side of the center
crease to create a ¼″- (6mm-) wide
spine and crease well.

3

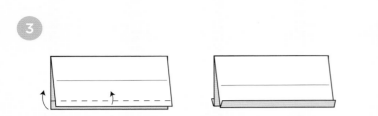

Valley fold the long sides of the paper into ½″ (13mm) hems. Be certain to keep the folds straight.

4

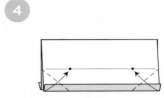

With the hem edges still folded, valley fold each bottom corner diagonally so the outside edge meets the nearest crease line. Turn the paper over and repeat on the other side.

7

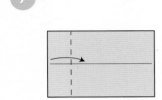

Valley fold the left edge 4½″ (11.5cm) to the right.

8

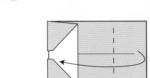

Bring the right edge over to meet the far left folded edge. Slip the edge just folded over into the triangle pockets directly underneath.

9

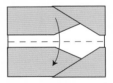

Fold the paper along the existing center crease. You should have 2 pockets on the inside and 2 on the outside.

tip: Insert the greetings into the pockets, and perhaps a few dollar bills!

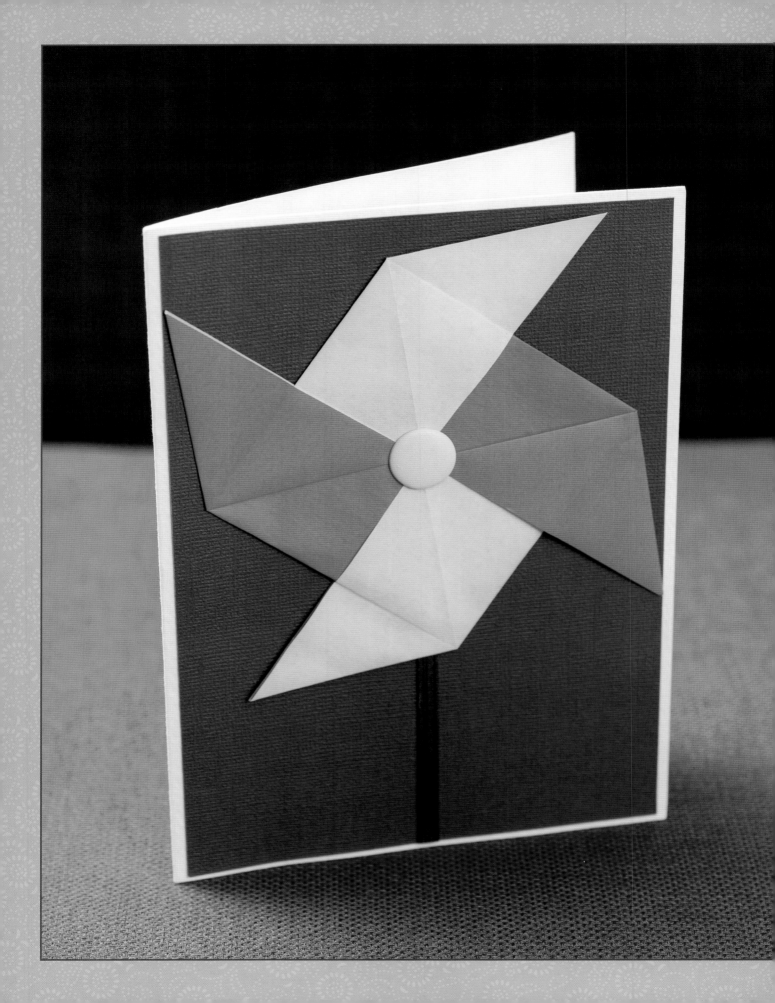

Pinwheel

I remember being mesmerized by pinwheels as a child. It was such a simple toy, yet many of my friends and I squealed with delight every time we watched it spin as we ran and let the wind create its magic. Folding a simple pinwheel shape out of a single sheet of paper will bring back fond memories and delight whoever receives it. This card can be made elegant or whimsical, depending on the occasion and your choice of paper and background. It works particularly well as a child's birthday card.

MATERIALS

1 sheet 6"- (15cm-) double-sided origami paper

Glue stick

Coordinating decorative card stock cut to 4½" x 6½" (11.5cm x 16.5cm)

1 blank greeting card, 5" x 7" (12.5cm x 18cm) when closed

Double-sided tape

⅛" (3mm) hole punch

Pronged metal brad or button brad

Mizuhiki ribbon or ¼"- (6mm-) wide ribbon

FINISHED SIZE

5" x 7" (12.5cm x 18cm) when closed

FOLD THE PINWHEEL

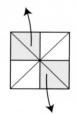

With the light-colored side facing up, valley fold the origami paper in half in both directions and unfold.

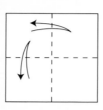

Valley fold 2 opposing corners to the center creases. Turn the paper over.

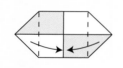

Fold the 2 remaining corners to the center.

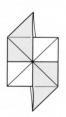

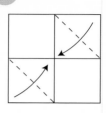

Pull out 2 opposing point flaps and flatten. Turn the paper over.

ASSEMBLE THE CARD

1 Glue the decorative card stock to the greeting card front.

2 Place the pinwheel onto the front of the card and adhere with double-sided tape.

3 Punch a hole through the center of the pinwheel, the card stock, and the card.

4 Attach brad or button brad through all layers of the card.

5 Using double-sided tape, attach a piece of ribbon at the bottom of the pinwheel to suggest a stick or wand.

3

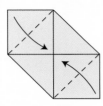

Fold the 2 remaining corners to the center creases.

4

 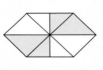

Fold the top and bottom corners to the center. Turn the paper over.

7

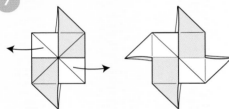

Pull out the remaining 2 flaps and you now have a pinwheel!

tip: Glue a sheet of decorative paper to the inside of the card to cover the brad spokes.

Woven Belt

This card has a simple but dramatic design, especially if you use contrasting double-sided paper. I used Japanese momigami paper, which is wrinkled on one side and has white kozo paper on the other. This card is sized to fit a standard size #10 business envelope (4⅛″ x 9½″ [10.5cm x 24cm]). To really make a statement, paint the envelope to match the card! You can send this for Father's Day, graduations, or congratulations. Write a special message, fold it into a little note, and tuck it between the strips of the belt for a personal touch.

MATERIALS

1 sheet black momigami paper, cut to 1¼″ x 21½″ (3cm x 54.5cm)

Bone folder

White glue

Glue applicator

FOR THE INSERT:

1 sheet of thin paper approximately 4″ x 8″ (10cm x 20cm)

1 sheet neutral-colored card stock cut to 8″ x 9½″ (20.5cm x 24cm)

1 sheet decorative paper or thin card stock cut to 3¾″ x 9¼″ (9.5cm x 23.5cm)

Double-sided tape

Acrylic paint and soft brush (optional)

FINISHED SIZE

4″ x 9½″ (10cm x 24cm)

FOLD THE WOVEN BELT

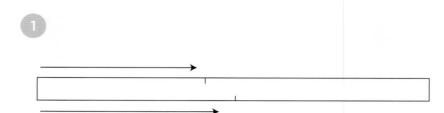

With the strip of momigami paper lying horizontally, white side up (or light side up, depending on your paper color), make a mark 9½″ (24cm) from the top left edge. Make a mark 10⅝″ (27cm) from the bottom left edge. These marks will be where you start your fold.

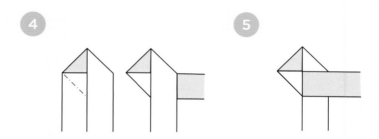

Rotate the paper so that the flat dark edge faces left. Mountain fold the left strip, laying it across the back of the other strip.

Tuck the right vertical strip under the left strip just folded

DECORATE AND ASSEMBLE THE CARD

1   Write a message on a thin sheet of paper, accordion fold it, and tuck it in to the belt. The accordion note can be tucked in anywhere along the length of the belt. Do not glue this down, as it is to be read by the recipient of the card.

2   Fold the card stock in half lengthwise. Your card will be sized to fit a standard business envelope, which you can decorate if desired to match the card.

3   Glue the decorative paper or card stock onto the front of the card.

4   Using double-sided tape, adhere the belt onto the card.

2

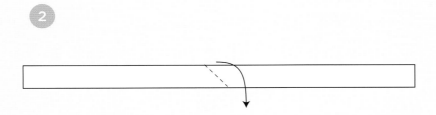

Fold the paper diagonally from the 9½" (24cm) mark to the 10⅝" (27cm) mark. The fold should be at a perfect 45-degree angle.

3

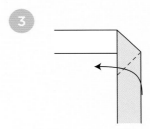

Valley fold the right strip to line it up against the inner edge of the left strip.

6

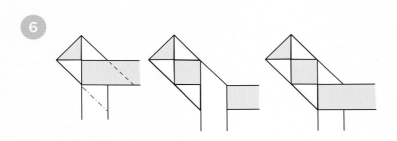

Alternate folding the strips as in steps 3, 4, and 5 throughout the length of the paper. Keep in mind that the black side will be in the center and the light side will be along the edges.

7

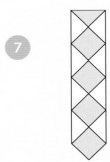

When you are finished folding, the belt should have 4½ black squares in the middle and 4 light triangles on each of the outer edges. Trim edges if needed. Crease the belt well using a bone folder and tack down any loose edges with a spot of glue.

tip: If you don't have contrasting double-sided paper for the woven belt, paint a color on the white side with acrylic paint. Let the paint dry thoroughly before folding.

Folded Frame

Based on a traditional origami fold, this frame holds a small photograph and can be used as a card embellishment if attached with a low-tack tape. Perfect for school photos old or new, my version of the card is made from vintage colored paper with an old graduation photo inserted. The tassel was attached to coordinate with the tassel in the photo. This card would also make a great baby announcement.

MATERIALS

1 sheet double-sided paper cut to 8″ (20.5cm) square

Glue stick or white glue

Sepia-toned photo or school photo

Colored card stock cut to 4¾″ x 6¾″ (12cm x 17cm)

1 blank greeting card, 5″ x 7″ (12.5cm x 18cm) when closed

1 sheet coordinating paper cut to 2¼″ x 6¾″ (5.5cm x 17cm) strip

Removable double-sided tape or poster tack

Tassel or other desired decorations

FINISHED SIZE

5″ x 7″ (12.5cm x 18cm) when closed

FOLD THE FRAME

 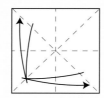

With the main color of the double-sided paper facing down, fold the paper in half vertically, horizontally, and in both diagonal directions. Unfold the paper and turn over.

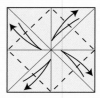

With the main color facing up, fold each corner to the center. Unfold the paper and turn over.

Do the same with the remaining 3 pockets.

  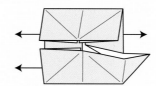

Fold the tip of the pocket to the center on all 4 flaps as shown.

Valley fold each inside triangle up so the point touches the outside edge and crease well. Apply a little glue to each flap so that they stay flat.

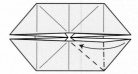 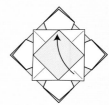

Cut the photo a little larger than the frame opening, which is about 1⅞″ (4.8cm) square, and slip it into the frame.

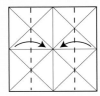

With the main color facing down, cupboard fold the left and right sides to the center crease.

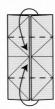

Cupboard fold the top and the bottom edges to the center.

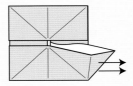

Open one pocket and pull out the corner. Flatten along the crease so that it points out at an angle.

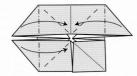

Open each corner, lay it over the top, and flatten to form a small square.

Fold the flaps pointing toward the center in half, facing outward.

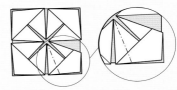

Mountain fold a raw edge on one point under to the flap's center line. Repeat with the other 7 flap edges.

ASSEMBLE THE CARD

1 Glue the piece of colored card stock onto the blank greeting card.

2 Glue the strip of decorative paper vertically along the center of the card.

3 Attach the folded frame using removable double-sided tape or poster tack.

Signature

A signature is a group of folded pages that are sewn together in stacks to make a traditional book. This card is called the Signature card because it is made up of simple folded elements and is glued together to create an unusual book-like card, but also because there are so many places to write or sign your name. You can make the card with any number of pages and color combinations.

MATERIALS

Several sheets 6"- (15cm-) square double-sided origami paper

Glue stick

¼"- (6mm-) wide coordinating ribbon

Double-sided tape

2 sheets decorative card stock cut to 2½" x 5½" (6.5cm x 14cm)

FINISHED SIZE

3" x 6" (7.5cm x 15cm)

FOLD FIRST PART OF SIGNATURE

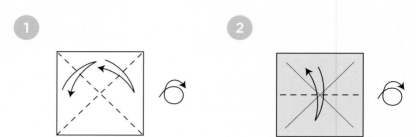

Fold one sheet of origami paper in half both ways diagonally and unfold after each fold. Turn the paper over.

Fold the sheet in half to create a rectangle crossing the diagonal crease. Unfold and turn over.

FOLD SECOND PART OF SIGNATURE

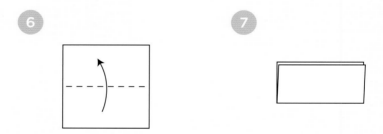

Fold another sheet of paper in half to create a rectangle.

Make three exactly alike.

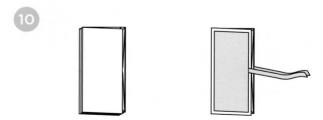

Glue the pages together along the front and back sides only, making sure all corners and edges are lined up perfectly.

3

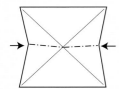

Push the sides together on the mountain folds.

4

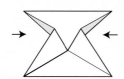

Collapse along the creases to create a triangle shape. This will be the inside of one signature.

5

Make three exactly alike.

ASSEMBLE THE SIGNATURE PAGES

8

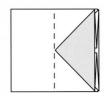

Open the rectangle sheet and glue the triangle-shaped sheet to the right side of the triangle, lining it up on the outer edges. Apply glue to the top of the triangle sheet, and fold the left side of the rectangle sheet back over.

9

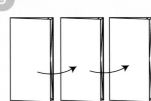

Stack the closed signatures on top of one another with the folded edges aligned in the same direction.

DECORATE THE CARD

1 Attach a strand of ribbon with double-sided tape to the front and back of the card, placing it about 1″ (2.3cm) from the edge, leaving about 6″ (15cm) to tie together at the card's opening edge.

2 Glue the sheets of card stock to the front and back covers over the ribbon.

Star

This simple fold is always fun to make and decorate. Folded elements are glued together to make a stunning display of shape and color, which will amaze your recipient when she or he opens the card. If you use double-sided paper, the finished card will be very dramatic. The bead slides up the ribbon so that you can open the card and display it as an ornament, making this a lovely choice for a holiday card.

MATERIALS

4 sheets (2 of each color) 6"–(15cm–) square double-sided scrapbook paper or origami paper

Glue stick

¼"– (6mm–) wide double-sided tape or glue

¼"– (6mm–) wide grosgrain ribbon

2 sheets decorative card stock cut to 2¾" (7cm) square

Corner rounder or small scissors

1 bead with a large hole (for ribbon to thread through)

Rubber stamp

Light–colored stamp pad

FINISHED SIZE

3" x 3" (7.5cm x 7.5cm)

FOLD THE STAR

 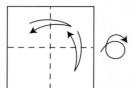 

With the patterned side down, valley fold a sheet of paper in half in both directions and unfold after each fold. Turn the paper over.

Stack all 4 folded sheets in the same direction (so they all open at the same corner) and glue together the sides that are touching. Let the glue dry completely. Make four in the same way.

The card will open up like a star.

2

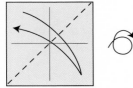

Valley fold the sheet in half once diagonally and crease well. Turn the paper over.

3

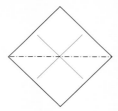

Push the sides together until the mountain folds touch.

4

Collapse each piece of folded paper along the crease lines so that you have 4 squares. Repeat steps 1–3 for the remaining 3 sheets of paper.

ASSEMBLE THE CARD

1 Apply double-sided tape diagonally across the front and back of the card, from the closed corner to the open corner.

2 Adhere 1 long piece of ribbon to the tape, wrapping the ribbon around the closed corner and extending the tails about 8″ (20.5cm) past the open corner on each side.

3 Center the card stock on both covers, on top of the ribbon, and glue it in place. For the example card, I used a corner rounder on 2 sides of the card stock to create rounded edges where the ribbon peeks through. If you can't find a corner rounder, just use small scissors to cut the rounded shape to make the edges less sharp.

4 Thread both ends of the ribbon through the bead. Slide the bead up and down to close and open the card.

Pop-Up Box with Fan-Out Card

The pop-up box folds flat for sending, but the receiver opens it out and up to find a surprise card inside. Heavyweight scrapbook paper gives the box its spring, and a ribbon belt holds the surprise inside. The double-sided paper makes the box both beautiful and functional.

MATERIALS

1 sheet medium- to heavyweight double-sided scrapbook paper cut to 9″ (23cm) square

Coordinating lightweight paper, which can be double sided or colored on both sides, cut to 5¾″ (14.5cm) square

2 sheets decorative card stock cut to 2⅜″ (6cm) square

Glue stick or white glue

Glue applicator

8″ (20.5cm) length 1″- (2.5cm-) wide contrasting ribbon

Double-sided tape

FINISHED SIZE

3¼″ (8cm) when closed

FOLD THE BOX

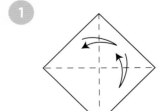

1. With the colored side down, fold the scrapbook paper in both diagonal directions and unfold after each fold.

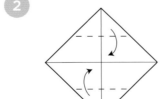

2. Valley fold the top and bottom corners to the center.

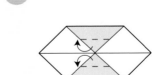

3. Mountain fold the top and bottom points in half and fold under.

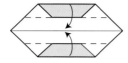

Valley fold the top and bottom edges in to meet the horizontal center crease.

Valley fold in half lengthwise and unfold.

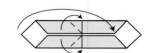

Make diagonal creases on the left side of the center crease and fold along the new diagonal creases so that the left point touches the right folded edges.

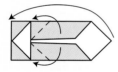

Make diagonal creases and fold right flap to go over to the left edge.

Valley fold all 3 triangle points on the right in to meet in the center.

Valley fold the left and right corners in to meet in the center.

FOLD THE FAN-OUT CARD

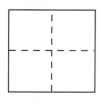

With the patterned side down, fold the 5¾" (14.5cm) square of paper horizontally and diagonally. Unfold and turn over.

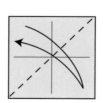

Fold diagonally and then unfold. Turn the paper over.

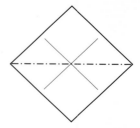

Push the sides together until the mountain folds touch.

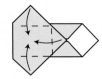

Valley fold all 3 triangle points on the left section to meet in the center.

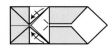

Valley fold the top and bottom corners on the left side of the left section to meet in the center.

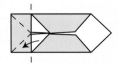

Valley fold the triangle point backwards to meet the left edge.

Valley fold the point you created in step 12 to meet the right edge.

Pull the triangle flaps to open the box.

Collapse the sides along the existing creases and fold into a flat square with 2 flaps on each side along the creases.

DECORATE THE CARD AND BOX

1 Glue a piece of card stock onto the front and back of the fan-out card. Decorate the inside of the card with paper, pictures, or a greeting. When done, fold the card closed and insert it into the bottom of the pop-up box.

2 Close the pop-up box and wrap a piece of ribbon around it, securing it at the back using double-sided tape. Attach the sheet of small card stock on top of the ribbon using double-sided tape. The ribbon and small card should slide on and off the box easily.

Kiss

Also known as the chatterbox, this interactive fold will surely put a smile on the face of whoever receives it. This whimsical card could be used for many occasions, such as Valentine's Day or a birthday. Send it to a friend and write, "It's been a while since we've chatted." It may take a few tries to master this fold, so I recommend practicing with plain paper first.

MATERIALS

1 sheet paper, colored on one side, cut to 8½" (21.5cm) square

White glue

Red acrylic paint

Small paintbrush

1 blank greeting card or heavyweight card stock cut to 5" x 10" (12.5cm x 25.5cm)

Lightweight colored card stock cut to 4½" (11.5cm) square

Decorative scrapbook paper cut to 4" (10cm) square

Double-sided tape

FINISHED SIZE

5" x 5" (12.5cm x 12.5cm)

FOLD THE LIPS

 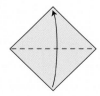

With the colored side facing up, fold the 8½" (21.5cm) paper in half diagonally.

 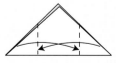

Mark the long edge of the folded triangle into thirds; the marks will be apart and 4" (10cm) in from each side.

With the top point aimed away from you, valley fold the right point over to meet the farthest mark on the left.

4

Valley fold the left triangle in half.

 5

Valley fold the top layer in half so that the raw edge meets the closest folded edge.

6

Fold the tip back. Crease well. Repeat steps 3–6 on right side. Crease well and unfold the entire square.

 10

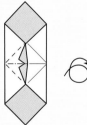

Make the valley and mountain creases as shown. Repeat steps 8–9 on the right side. Turn over.

 11

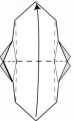

Fold in half so that the bottom point meets the top point.

 12

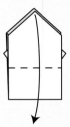

Fold the top layer down so that just the triangle extends beyond the bottom edge.

 15

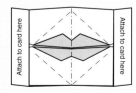

Glue the 2 previously folded rectangle edges together on both flaps. Hold a flap in each hand, move them back and forth, and watch the lips move!

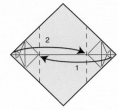

Valley fold the right side along the existing crease line so that the point touches the left vertical crease. Then fold the left point to touch the right folded edge. It will lay over the previously folded point.

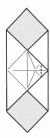

Fold right tip back to touch first crease.

Start folding backwards, but don't crease all the way.

Fold the top layer of the bottom edge in half.

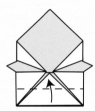

Fold the top layer of the bottom edge in half again. Repeat steps 12–14 on the top edge.

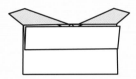

This is how it looks when closed.

DECORATE AND ASSEMBLE THE CARD

1 Lightly paint the lips with red acrylic paint. Let dry completely.

2 If you're using heavyweight card stock instead of a blank greeting card, fold the card stock in half.

3 Glue the colored card stock to the front of the card.

4 Glue the decorative scrapbook paper to the card stock.

5 Apply a strip of double-sided tape to each of the outer flaps on the folded lips, and fold the lips flat.

6 Attach the folded lips on the inside of the card about 1″ (2.5cm) from center fold on each side.

7 Open and close the card to make the lips open and close. It is sure to open up an interesting conversation.

Crane

The crane is well known as a symbol of longevity and peace. Its long neck and wide wingspan symbolize long life and perseverance. This lovely crane card is perfect for wedding invitations and anniversary announcements, and makes an elegant and unique memento to use as table decorations at parties and celebrations.

MATERIALS

1 sheet medium-weight decorative paper cut to 7½" x 12" (19cm x 30.5cm)

Decorative paper cut to 2" x 5½" (5cm x 14cm)

PVA, heavy-bodied white glue, or double-sided tape

FINISHED SIZE

3¾" x 5" (9.5cm x 12.5cm)

FOLD THE CRANE

 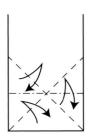

With the 7½" x 12" (19cm x 30.5cm) sheet of paper oriented portrait style and the colored side down, diagonally valley fold each bottom corner so the bottom edge aligns with the far side, then mountain fold horizontally at the crease intersection and unfold.

Push the sides in and collapse so that you have a triangle with 2 flaps on either side. Make creases on the top flaps by valley folding to the center of the triangle, then unfold.

Valley fold the right corner flap so that the 2 top flaps lie on the left side.

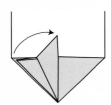

Valley fold the top flap on the left in half diagonally again so the point comes to the center and forms a tip.

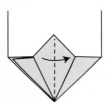

Open the tip and flatten it on the crease lines, then unfold to the right.

Repeat steps 4 and 5 for the right side flap.

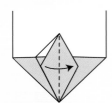
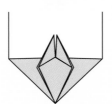

Fold the top layer in half. Repeat steps 7 and 8 on the opposite flap.

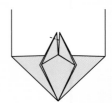

Fold a corner down on one point to create the beak, then reverse the fold by folding inside so that a mountain fold is on each side of a valley fold.

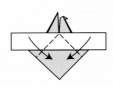

Valley fold the top accordion edges down diagonally to meet in the center. Crease well.

Fold the 2" x 5½" (5cm x 14cm) strip of decorative paper in half lengthwise to make a 1"- (2.5cm-) wide band, and glue down the folds.

Wrap the folded strip around the bottom of the crane and glue or tape the 2 ends of the band together. The band will slide off to allow the card to open.

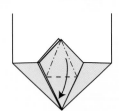 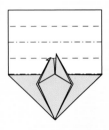

 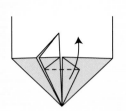

Valley fold the top point down to meet the bottom point along the mountain and valley crease lines. Open and flatten along the crease lines.

Fold the point just folded back up along the crease line.

 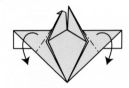 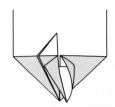

Divide the remaining unfolded sheet into fourths and accordion fold at the top raw edge down to the folded edge of the crane.

Fold the accordion layers backward so the edges meet at the center. Turn the paper over.

tip: When you're done folding the crane, glue down all the raw edges (except for the folded note card section) to make the crane lay flat.

Accordion

This card is made up of six folded sheets of paper, which are linked together to make an accordion card with pockets for photos. This card fits perfectly into the Folded Box (page 74)!

MATERIALS

6 sheets 6"- (15cm-) square scrapbook paper or origami paper

6 sheets card stock (or photos) cut to 2⅞" (7.3cm) square

5 sheets of lightweight card stock cut to 2⅛" (5.4cm) square

Double-sided tape

¼"- (6mm-) wide grosgrain ribbon

Glue stick

Coordinating paper or card stock for front and back covers cut to 2¾" (7cm) square

FINISHED SIZE

3" x 3" (7.5cm x 7.5cm)

FOLD THE ACCORDION SQUARES

 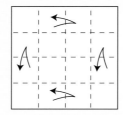 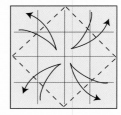

With the colored or patterned side down, fold one of the 6" (15cm) squares of paper into 16 equal sections and unfold after each fold. Turn the paper over.

Valley fold all 4 corners to the center, then unfold. Turn the paper over (patterned side down).

ASSEMBLE THE CARD

Insert a 2⅞" (7.3cm) square of card stock or a photo in each unit by inserting the corners into the 4 pockets.

Fold the 2⅛" (5.4cm) squares of card stock in half diagonally. Crease back and forth several times to make them flexible. These will be the "joints" for your accordion frame card.

DECORATE THE CARD

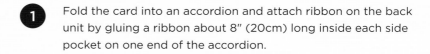

Fold the card into an accordion and attach ribbon on the back unit by gluing a ribbon about 8" (20cm) long inside each side pocket on one end of the accordion.

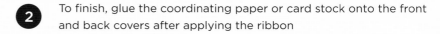

To finish, glue the coordinating paper or card stock onto the front and back covers after applying the ribbon

3

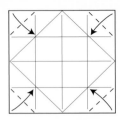

Fold all 4 corners to the first intersected creases.

4

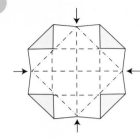

Bring the center of each raw edge in toward the center of the square and down, collapsing in along the existing creases.

5

Flatten the unit and crease well. Fold all 6 squares of paper exactly the same.

8

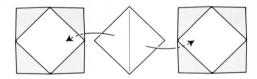

Apply double-sided tape to one face of the joints, ⅛" (3mm) in each direction away from the crease line. Lay the units side by side and insert the joints into the side pockets.

Folded Box

Presentation is everything, and this box is a joy to fold as well as to give. I have always been particularly fascinated by folded boxes because they are functional as well as beautiful. This box, which holds the Accordion card (page 70) perfectly, can also be used to present a small gift or as a candy container. I have folded this box a few hundred times, and every time I slide the units together I am delighted with the results.

MATERIALS	FINISHED SIZE
8 assorted sheets 6"- (15cm-) square origami or scrapbook paper	3¼" (8.3cm) square

FOLD THE TOP

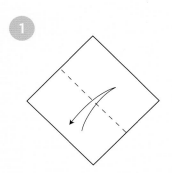

1

With the colored side facing down, valley fold one sheet of paper in half and unfold. Orient the paper diamond style with the crease positioned as shown.

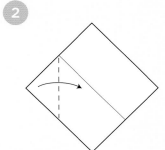

2

Valley fold the left point so the edge meets the center crease line.

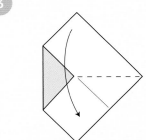

3

Fold the paper in half diagonally (top point to bottom point).

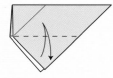

 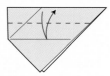

 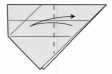

Make a crease on the upper layer by folding the bottom point to meet the top edge, then unfold.

Make a crease on the upper layer by folding the bottom point to meet the top edge, then unfold.

Fold the top edge down to meet the crease you just made and unfold.

Fold the right point over by folding the top folded edge in half. Unfold.

 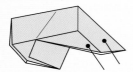

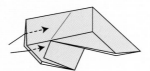

After the 4 units are folded, slide each unit's left point into the neighboring unit's right pocket until they all lock together. This step takes a little practice and patience, but it's well worth the effort when finished!

 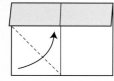

 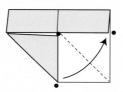

Fold the bottom left corner up so that the corner and right edge meet the center crease.

Fold the bottom right section in half diagonally and run your finger up to the first (horizontal) crease, making a diagonal crease.

Drop the top left side down; the 2 sides will come up. Repeat steps 10–15 with 3 more sheets of paper to make the remaining units.

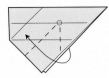

Fold the bottom point so that the right edge meets the parallel diagonal crease, and run your finger up along the fold until you meet the uppermost crease.

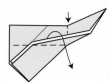

With your finger still holding the intersection, drop the right part down to create one side of the box. Crease well. Repeat steps 1–8 with 3 more sheets of paper to make the remaining walls.

FOLD THE BASE

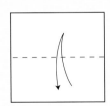

With the colored side down, valley fold one sheet of paper in half horizontally and unfold.

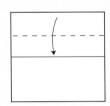

Valley fold the top half down to the center crease line.

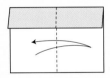

With the folded edge facing up, valley fold the paper in half in the other direction, making sure the top folded edges are aligned. Unfold.

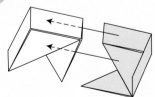

After the 4 units are folded, slide each unit's right side into the neighboring unit's left pocket until they all lock together.

tips:

- The units will slide together more easily if you use smooth-finished papers.

- To make the bottom of the box a little sturdier, insert a piece of card stock cut slightly smaller than the inside dimensions of the box.

- Insert the Accordion card (page 70) into the box to create a very special gift.

Secret Message

I designed this card while I was at an event and participating in a raffle. Once the numbers had all been called, I started to fold my raffle ticket and created this fun but easy-to-make card. It is stunning made with double-sided paper, and a ribbon ties it all together.

MATERIALS

1 sheet heavyweight double-sided scrapbook paper cut to 6″ x 12″ (15cm x 30.5cm)

1 sheet card stock cut to 5¾″ (14.5cm) square

½″- (13mm-) wide satin ribbon

Double-sided tape

FINISHED SIZE

3″ x 6″ (7.5cm x 15cm)

FOLD THE CARD

 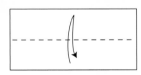

Orient the paper landscape style with the patterned side—which is the side you want on the outside—down. Fold the paper in half lengthwise and unfold.

 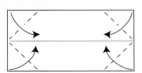

Fold all 4 corners in diagonally to meet the center crease line.

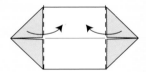

Where the corner folds end, valley fold the right and left sides to meet in the center.

Fold in half lengthwise and crease well. You will now have pockets to insert a greeting.

Insert the card stock, and fold the sides together again.

Attach the ribbon using the double-sided tape, wrapping the ribbon around the front, spine, and back of the card, and tie the ribbon to close the card.

tip: Write a secret message under the triangle flaps of the folded card.

Jacob's Ladder

I was fascinated by this fold when, at a San Francisco origami conference, origami designer Yami Yamauchi shared with me his version of the Jacob's Ladder, which he called the Magic Wallet. Based on the classic wooden toy, this card appears to have no end and will truly amuse the recipient as he or she folds it back and forth. This magical card can be simple or whimsical, depending on the paper you select. It is important to use fairly thin, smooth paper, such as bond or copy paper, which is available at office supply stores.

MATERIALS

3 sheets 8½" x 11" (21.5cm x 28cm) paper, 2 of one color and 1 of a contrasting color

4 sheets card stock cut to 2½" x 4¾" (6.5cm x 12cm)

Glue stick

FINISHED SIZE

2⅞" x 5⅛" (7.3cm x 13cm)

FOLD THE CARDS

 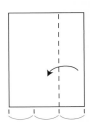

Divide one of the matching-color sheets of paper lengthwise into 3 equal sections, each approximately 2¾" (7cm) wide, and valley fold the right third over the left side of the paper with the paper oriented portrait style.

 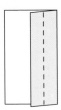

Fold back the top layer to the right folded edge.

 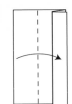

Fold the left third to the outer right edge.

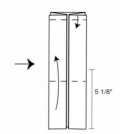 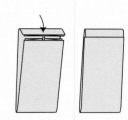

4 Fold the top layer to the left folded edge. With the already folded edges facing up, fold 1 narrow end down ¾" (19mm).

5 Fold the bottom edge up to meet the top folded edge.

5 1/8"

6 Tuck the short folded edge into the pockets of the opposite long folded edge. Repeat steps 1–6 to fold the other sheet of the same color the same way. You will have 2 units measuring 2¾" x 5⅛" (7cm x 13cm).

INSERT THE BANDS

 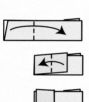 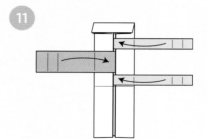 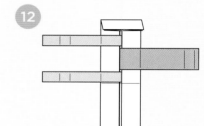

10 Valley fold the left third to meet the folded edge of the right third. Valley fold the section just folded back to meet the left folded edge.

11 Open one of the main pages and tuck the 2 thin bands into the right fold. Tuck the thick band into the left fold between the 2 thin bands.

12 Fold the bands along the existing valley folds over the page.

16 Open and close the card in a back-and-forth motion and adjust the band so that it opens and closes easily. When the card is completely closed, you will have a plain front and back cover with 3 bands on the inside. When you open it from the front or the back, the bands will appear like magic!

FOLD THE BANDS

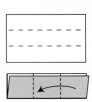

Cut the remaining (contrasting) sheet in half crosswise to make 2 sheets measuring 5½" x 8½" (14cm x 21.5cm). Fold one sheet length-wise into thirds to make a strip that is 1⅞" x 8½" (4.8cm x 21.5cm). Then fold it into thirds crosswise.

Cut one of the 5½" x 8½" sheets in half again into 2 sheets measuring 2¾" x 8½" (7cm x 21.5cm). Fold the 2 smaller sheets in half length-wise, then fold them into thirds crosswise.

Prepare all 3 bands the same way: Unfold the left third. Valley fold the right third back to meet the outside folded edge. Turn the folded strips over.

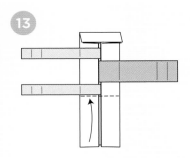

Fold up the main page bottom along previous crease and lock by tucking into the top pocket covering the bands.

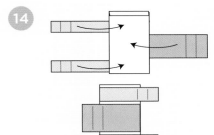

Fold the bands flat over the top of the main page.

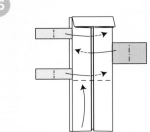

Keep the bands in place on the first page and open up the second page and lay on top. Lock by tucking into the top pocket covering the bands.

DECORATE THE CARD

1 Insert 2 pieces of card stock into the bands on the inside of the card.

2 Glue the remaining 2 pieces of card stock to the outside front and back of the card.

Postcard Holder

Adapted from the traditional Japanese folded tissue holder, this card holds a 4″ x 6″ (10cm x 15cm) photo or postcard. Perfect for baby announcements or mementos of vacation, the card can be unfolded to store more postcards or photos. Double-sided paper makes the holder especially dramatic, and acid-free scrapbook paper is great because photos will not be damaged even if they are stored in the holder for an extended period of time.

MATERIALS

1 sheet 12″ x 12″ (30.5cm x 30.5cm)
double-sided medium-weight
scrapbook paper

FINISHED SIZE

4″ x 6⅛″ (10cm x 15cm)

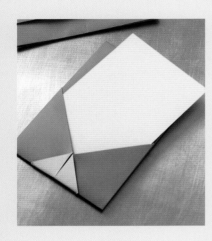

FOLD THE CARD

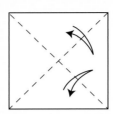

With the dominant-color
side down, fold and unfold the
paper in half diagonally in both
directions. Orient the paper
diamond style.

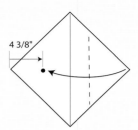

Measure 4⅜″ (10cm) from the left
point and fold the right point to
that measurement.

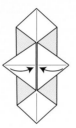

Fold the 2 outer side points
toward the center.

Valley fold the top layer on each
side again and tuck the points
inward.

3

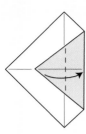

Valley fold the point just folded back along the center crease below.

 4

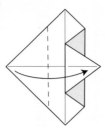

Valley fold the left point to lie perfectly on top of the folded right point.

5

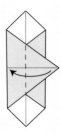

Valley fold the top layer back along the center crease.

 8

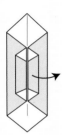

Open the right flap and refold on the existing crease to tuck the point around and under the left flap. Doing this will secure the holder.

9

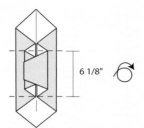

6 1/8"

Fold the top and bottom points of the paper so that there is a 6⅛" (15.6cm) space between the folds. Turn the paper over.

10

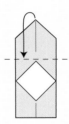

Tuck one point into the pocket created by the opposite point.

Dos-à-Dos

Dos-à-dos is French for "back-to-back." This card is really two cards in one, bound together by a cover. Stitched into the cover are signatures in which you can have as many pages as you wish. There is plenty of room for poems, pictures, greetings, or autographs. For a wedding or anniversary, this card could contain stories of the couple, with the special date printed on the cover.

MATERIALS

1 sheet card stock cut to 10½" x 5½"
(26.5cm x 14cm)

5 sheets colored copy paper cut to
5¼" x 6⅜" (13.3cm x 16.2cm)

Blunt sewing needle for punching
stitching holes

24" (61cm) length ⅛"– (3mm–) wide
woven ribbon or thin yarn

5 sheets different colored copy paper
cut 5¼" x 6⅜" (13.3cm x 16.2cm)

White glue or glue stick

2 sheets decorative paper cut to
3" x 5" (7.5cm x 12.5cm)

FINISHED SIZE

5½" x 3½" (14cm x 9cm)

FOLD THE CARD

 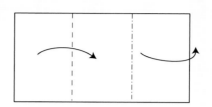

Fold the card stock into crosswise thirds. Crease the folds well.

Fold 5 sheets of copy paper in one of the colors in half crosswise and punch 3 small holes, about 2" (5cm) apart, in the crease through all the sheets.

 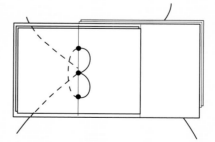

Repeat steps 3–5 for the other valley fold and the other color of copy paper.

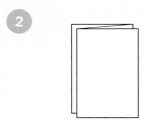

2

If you stand the paper up, you will see there are 2 valleys going in opposite directions. This is where you will stitch the signatures into your card.

4

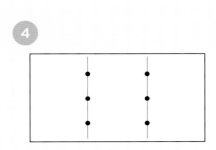

Punch 3 small holes in one valley crease of the folded card stock, using the holes in the copy paper as a guide.

5

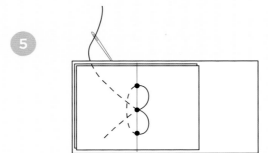

Place the signature into the punched valley crease. Using the needle and thin ribbon, pass the ribbon down through the center hole from the outside of the card and paper signatures, then go up through one of the other holes and out the back, crossing over the center hole and back down through the remaining hole. Bring the needle back up through the center hole and tie the ends to secure.

7

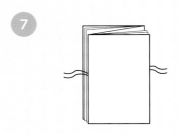

Fold along the crease lines.

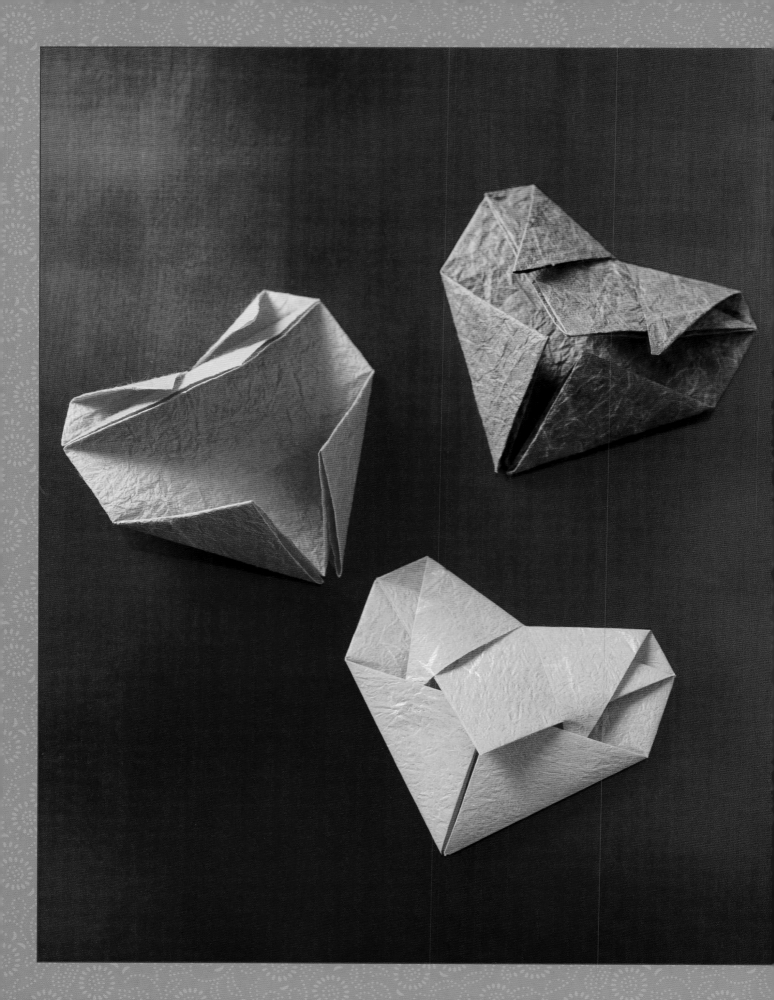

From the Heart

This heart-shaped card and envelope in one looks much harder to make than it actually is. The unique shape makes a great Valentine's Day greeting and is perfect for a love note. Send it to that special someone and insert a heartfelt message that will never be forgotten.

MATERIALS

1 sheet 8½" x 11" decorative paper
(21.5cm x 28cm)

FINISHED SIZE

4" x 4¼" (10cm x 11cm)

FOLD THE HEART

 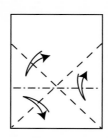

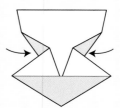

With the desired exterior color side down and the paper oriented portrait style, valley fold the bottom corners up diagonally so the bottom edge meets the side, unfolding the first fold before you make the next fold. Unfold the second fold. At the intersection of the creases, mountain fold horizontally.

Bring the mountain folds together to collapse into a flat triangle with flaps on both the front and the back.

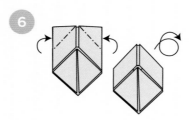

Mountain fold the top corners backward so the edges meet on the reverse side. Turn the paper over.

Valley fold the bottom triangle layer as far as it will go.

3

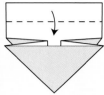

Valley fold the top edge to meet the raw edge on the triangle.

4

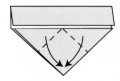

Valley fold the top-layer triangle flaps to meet at the bottom point.

5

Valley fold the right and left sides to meet at the center.

8

Valley fold the remaining bottom points at an angle so their tips lie over the folded edge. Tuck the tips under the right and left pockets and turn over.

9

Tuck the points into the pockets on either side of the triangle to hold the heart together.

10

Crease all folds well and place between heavy books to make the folds strong.

tip: Unfold the entire heart to reveal a greeting inside. In this card, I stamped a phrase in black ink on lightweight paper, cut it to 1½" x 4¼" (3.8cm x 11cm), and glued it inside the card.

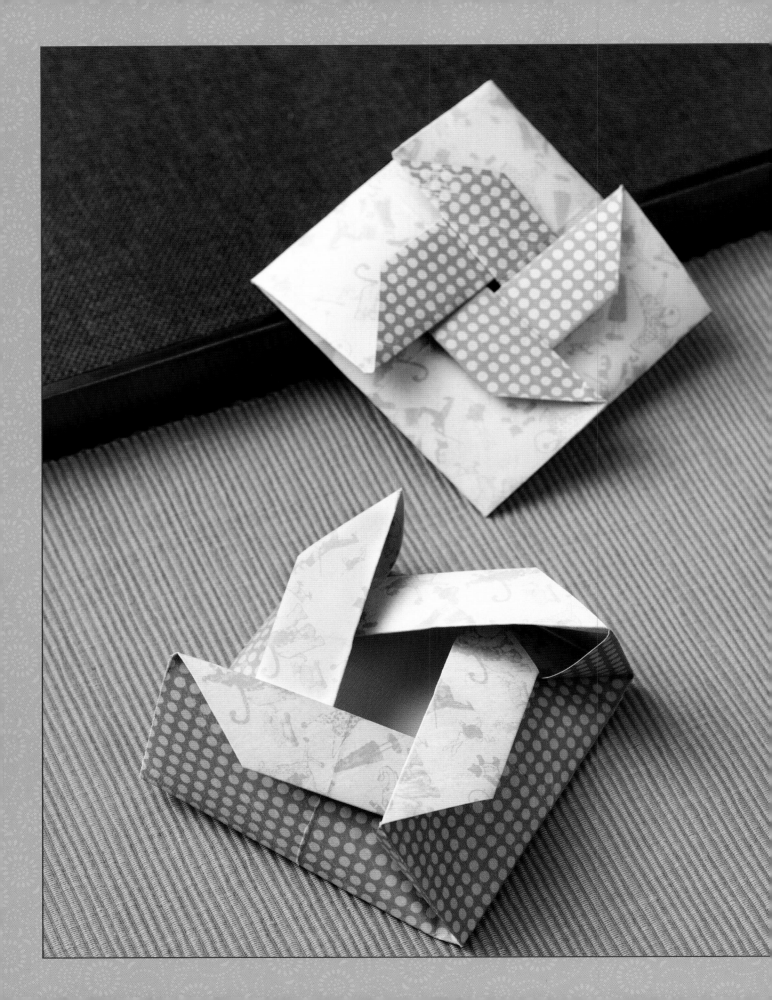

Tato Puzzle

A Tato is a folded paper purse that originated in Japan and holds small items such as needles and thread or postage stamps. This card opens much like a puzzle, and when unfolded it reveals the message inside.

MATERIALS

1 sheet double-sided scrapbook paper cut to 8½" (21.5cm) square

Glue stick

2 sheets of coordinating card stock cut to 3⅞" (9.8cm) square

FINISHED SIZE

4" x 4" (10cm x 10cm)

FOLD THE CARD

1

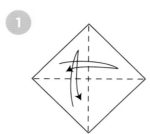

With the paper oriented diamond style and the dominant-color side facing down, fold the paper diagonally in both directions, then unfold.

2

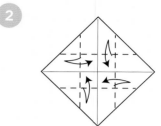

Valley fold all 4 corners so each crease is 2" (5cm) away from the center, making sure your crease lines are equally spaced apart on all sides. Unfold.

6

Valley fold the point just folded at the center crease, then fold the point under.

7

Fold the top point down to meet the bottom edge.

11

Fold the left top flap out.

12

Make the bottom left crease a mountain fold and the top left crease a valley fold, and tuck the edge underneath the closest folded flap. Your card is now finished, with little flaps that tuck into each other to close.

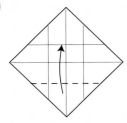

3

Fold the bottom corner (facing you) up to meet the farthest crease line.

4

Fold the point back down at the center crease, then fold the point under.

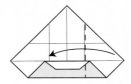

5

Valley fold the right point to the farthest left crease.

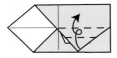

8

Fold the point back up at the center crease, then fold the point under.

9

Valley fold the left point to meet the farthest right folded edge.

10

Valley fold the point back to the left crease, then fold the point under.

ASSEMBLE THE CARD

1 Open the card while preserving the previous point folds and glue a $3\frac{7}{8}$" (9.8cm) sheet of card stock to the inside center, where the message will be.

2 Close the card along the previous folds and glue the remaining piece of the card stock to the back to make it more sturdy. This also gives you another place to write a greeting.

3 To open the card again, gently lift the corners up and out. To close, fold the points back in and tuck the last corner underneath the corner next to it.

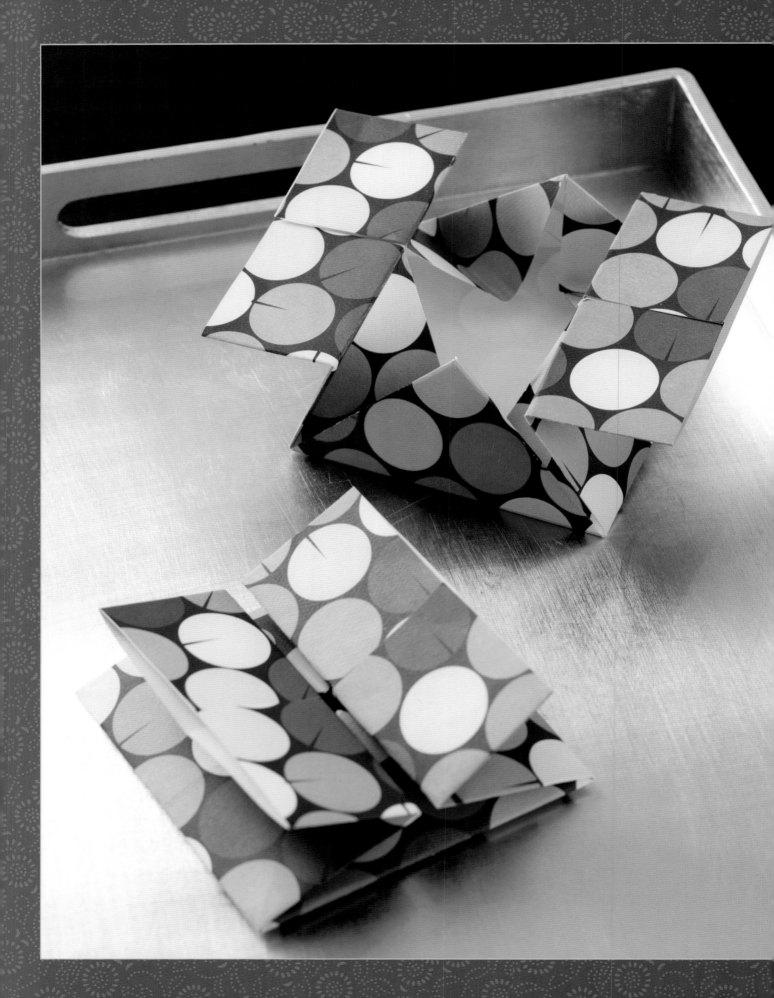

Pop-Out

This card lies flat for mailing and is three-dimensional when popped open, revealing a surprise greeting inside. There is room for other flat surprises as well, such as money or concert tickets. Opening and closing the card is easy: Just pull the rectangle flaps to open, and when closing the card, insert the triangle flaps back under the rectangle flaps.

MATERIALS

1 sheet double-sided scrapbook paper cut to 8½" x 12" (21.5cm x 30.5cm)

1 sheet plain paper cut to 3½" x 3¼" (9cm x 8.3cm)

Glue

1 sheet card stock cut to 4" x 3¾" (10cm x 9.5cm)

FINISHED SIZE

4¼" x 4¼" (11cm x 11cm) when closed

FOLD THE CARD

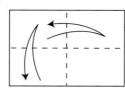

With the paper oriented landscape style and the dominant-color side facing down, fold the paper in half from top to bottom, then side to side, and unfold.

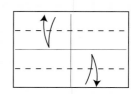

Fold the outside edges on both lengthwise sides to the center crease and unfold.

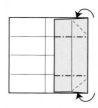

Fold both corners inside.

Valley fold the flap back to meet the outer edge and crease well.

You will now have 2 triangle points. Tuck the point under the rectangular flap on each side.

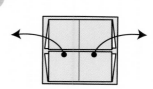

Pull out at ● so inside will pop out.

3

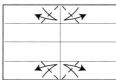

Make creases at a 45-degree angle to meet the intersecting creases at the top and bottom.

4

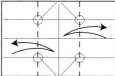

Valley fold both sides vertically at the points where the 45-degree creases meet the horizontal creases. Unfold.

5

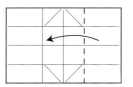

Valley fold the right side to the farthest existing crease and refold the diagonal folds on the outer-most left corners.

8

Fold the left side along the existing crease line and make 2 diagonal folds on the outermost right corners, just as you did on the other side.

9

Push both corners in, reversing some of the folds so that you have an almost square flap on top of the 2 triangle layers.

10

Valley fold the flap back to meet the outer edge and crease well.

13

The inside dimensions are 4⅛" (10.5cm). Make a greeting on the plain paper and glue it to the card stock. Insert the greeting into the center of the card and fold it closed. This card pops up nicely when you lift the top layer flaps and closes very easily using the existing creases.

Simple Fold

This cute card and envelope in one has a clever locking closure and two inside pockets to tuck little notes or photos into. Your choice of paper can make this practical, easy-to-fold card elegant or whimsical.

MATERIALS

1 sheet decorative paper cut to 8½" (21.5cm) square

2 sheets card stock (or photos) cut to 2⅞" x 3⅞" (7.3cm x 9.8cm)

FINISHED SIZE

4" x 3⅟₁₆" (10cm x 7.8cm)

FOLD THE CARD

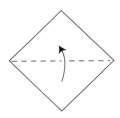

With the colored side down, fold the paper in half diagonally.

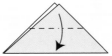

Fold 1 corner flap down so that it meets the center of the folded edge.

Fold the right side over a third of the way across the diagonal fold, which will be 4" (10cm) in from the point.

Fold the left side over the side you just folded so that the point meets the right folded edge.

Fold the tip of the left side backward so it touches the left corner and makes a triangular flap.

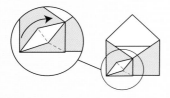

Separate the small triangular flap, pull the bottom corner up, and press it flat to make a small diamond in the middle.

Fold the top point down and tuck into the diamond shaped pocket. Open the envelope and insert the card stock or photos into the front and back pockets.

ENVELOPES

Simple

When creating your own cards you may not have a matching envelope available, so this is the perfect solution and can be used for just about any shape or size of card. The basic formula for most odd-sized cards is to cut your envelope paper double the width and length of the folded card. You can change the width and angle of the fold of this envelope, and it will turn out perfectly every time!

MATERIALS

1 sheet 8½" x 11" (21.5cm x 28cm) paper

FINISHED SIZE

Approximately 3¾" x 5⅝" (9.5cm x 14.3cm)

tip: This envelope is great for mass-mailing printed announcements. Just secure the envelope with a piece of tape or a sticker and address the front side.

FOLD THE ENVELOPE

 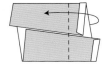

Place the paper colored side down with portrait-style orientation. Fold a ½" (13mm) border along the long side of the paper.

 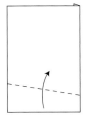

Make a diagonal fold at the bottom edge of the paper. The fold height and the fold angle are up to you, but make sure the fold doesn't pass more than halfway up the paper.

 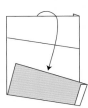

Fold the top edge diagonally to meet the bottom raw edge.

Fold the right side vertically so that the folded edges are aligned along both the top and bottom. The width of the fold is up to you.

Fold the left side vertically so that the folded edges are aligned and tuck into the folded raw edge about ½" (13mm).

Insert the flaps into the pocket. The thin white band is perfect for writing an address.

Classic

This envelope has a more traditional look and makes a beautiful card holder. The paper is folded in such a way that the top flap tucks into the bottom edge to lock the envelope in place. You can choose from a variety of decorative papers in a size that matches your greeting card. Begin with an A4-size paper, a standard size in Europe and Japan that can be purchased on the Internet. It is approximately 8¼″ x 11⅝″ (21cm x 29.5cm). This envelope also works with 8½″ x 12″ (21.5cm x 30.5cm) or 7″ x 10″ (18cm x 25.5cm) paper, but will not work with U.S. standard 8½″ x 11″ (21.5cm x 28) paper.

MATERIALS

1 sheet 8¼" x 11⅝" (21cm x 29.5cm; A4 size) paper

FINISHED SIZE

6" x 4¾" (15cm x 12cm)

FOLD THE ENVELOPE

 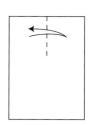

With paper oriented portrait style and the decorative side facing down, make a short vertical crease perpendicular to the top short edge to find the center.

 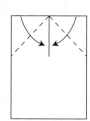

Valley fold the 2 top corners down to meet the small center crease.

 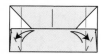

 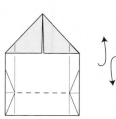

At the bottom edge, valley fold the corners starting where the bottom crease line meets the creases from step 5 and ending at the first raw edge. Unfold.

Unfold the paper, leaving the top triangle flap folded.

 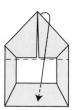

Valley fold the top triangle flap along the existing crease line and tuck the point into the bottom edge to secure.

The envelope will lock in place without the use of adhesive!

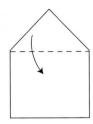

Valley fold the top triangular flap down along the raw edges of the corners you just folded.

Valley fold the bottom edge up about 2⅝" (6.7cm) at the triangle point to cover the flap.

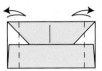

Valley fold the right and left sides inward so the raw edges meet the intersection of the rectangle flap and the triangle flap. Each side will have a hem about 1" (2.5cm) wide. Unfold.

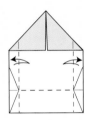

Valley fold the 1" (2.5cm) outside hems and crease well, then unfold.

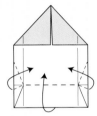

Valley fold the bottom edge back up along the existing crease line and push in the bottom part of the hems along the diagonal creases to collapse them under the bottom flap, leaving the upper hem lying flat.

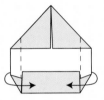

Valley fold the outside hem along the existing crease line on both sides.

CLASSIC   113

Square with Pocket

This easy-to-make square-shaped envelope was a real hit when I demonstrated it on *The Carol Duvall Show.* It has many uses: When folded, there is an outside pocket into which you can tuck tickets, a note, or a fortune. The inside can be decorated or written on before folding, and it is easy to put back together after it's unfolded. This envelope will also work well with a sheet of 7″ x 10″ (18cm x 25.5cm) or 11″ x 17″ (28cm x 43cm) paper to create different sizes.

MATERIALS

1 sheet 8½″ x 11″ (21.5cm x 28cm) paper

FINISHED SIZE

Approximately 3¾″ x 5⅝″ (9.5cm x 14.3cm)

FOLD THE ENVELOPE

1

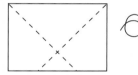

With the paper oriented landscape style and the colored side down, valley fold the right bottom corner all the way up to meet the top edge and unfold, then fold and unfold the left bottom corner in the same way. Turn the paper over.

2

Mountain fold horizontally at the intersection of the creases just made and unfold. Turn the paper over.

3

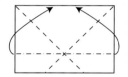

Push the center crease down and the mountain folds on each side will pop up a little.

1

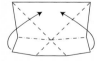

Bring the mountain folds to meet in the center and flatten the triangle pocket at the bottom.

2

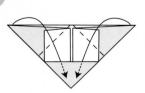

Fold the right and left outer points to meet at the bottom, making sure the sides line up.

3

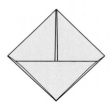

Tuck both points into the triangle pockets.

Square with Tabs

I love this envelope because of the clever interlocking tabs that keep it closed. And the square shape with a dimensional top is fun and quite unique. It is not difficult to fold, but the receiver will think it is!

MATERIALS

1 sheet 8½" x 12" (21.5cm x 30.5cm) paper

FINISHED SIZE

4" x 4" (10cm x 10cm)

FOLD THE ENVELOPE

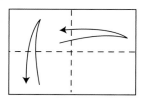

With the paper oriented landscape style and the colored side down, valley fold in half in both directions, then unfold. You will have 4 equal rectangles.

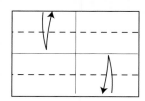

Valley fold the top and bottom edges to meet the center crease and unfold.

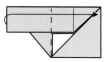

Fold the left and right long flaps back on themselves so the end of the flap meets the point at which the flap meets the diagonal edge.

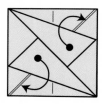
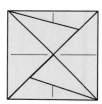

Tuck the tabs into the pockets to close the envelope.

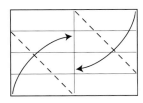

Valley fold the left bottom corner to the center vertical crease.

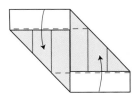

Valley fold the top right corner to the center vertical crease.

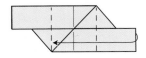

Fold the top and bottom edges along the existing crease lines to meet at the center.

Fold the top flap at an angle, starting at the left top corner, and bring the edge to meet the center diagonal center. Fold the bottom flap at a parallel angle, starting from the bottom right corner, and bring the edge to meet that of the top flap.

Elegant

This versatile envelope has an unusual shape, and the proportions will be different depending on which orientation you use to start the fold—perfect for odd-sized cards. This envelope has a sturdy locking flap and looks dimensional when finished. Use strong but fairly lightweight paper, or the finished project may be too thick.

MATERIALS

1 sheet 8½" x 12" (21.5cm x 30.5cm) paper

FINISHED SIZE

4¼" x 5" (11cm x 12.5cm)

FOLD THE ENVELOPE

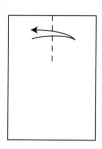

With the paper oriented portrait style and the colored side down, make a 3" (7.5cm) vertical crease at the top edge to find the center.

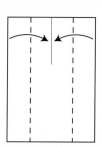

Fold the outside edges to the center.

Fold the bottom edge up so the crease touches the point just folded. Unfold.

With the bottom edges slightly open, tuck the top triangle flap inside.

MAIL THE ENVELOPE

Seal with a sticker.

Address and send!

3

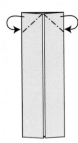

Fold the 2 top corners so the edges meet the center crease on the back side.

4

Fold the top edges at an angle so the folds from the previous step meet the center crease, and let the triangle flaps from the back come out. You will now have a divided square at the top.

5

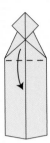

Fold the entire top point down along the bottom of the angle creases made in the previous step.

8

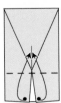

Bring up the 2 edges on the bottom and tuck them into the point.

9

Make a diagonal valley crease on both remaining raw edges and reverse to a mountain fold. Tuck both corners inside to finish.

Resources

The following is a list of suppliers and resources for paper, tools, other supplies, and inspiration. All of these products are available in art supply and craft stores, as well as online.

Paper and Craft Supplies

ALUMICOLOR

I highly recommend using a straight-edge ruler for cutting straight lines and getting accurate sizes for your paper folding. Check out the AlumiCutter, which comes in many different colors and sizes.

www.alumicolor.com

ARTWISE AMAZING PAPER

A4-sized papers

186 Enmore Road

Enmore, NSW 2042

www.amazingpaper.com.au

DANIEL SMITH

Acrylic paints, artist materials, and decorative papers.

800–426–7923

www.danielsmith.com

GOLDEN ARTIST COLORS

Manufacturer of acrylic paint and materials for professional refinishers and artists.

www.goldenpaints.com

GRAPHIC PRODUCTS CORPORATION

Decorative papers from all over the world

www.gpcpapers.com

JO-ANN FABRICS AND CRAFTS

Scrapbook papers and supplies. There are many locations throughout the U.S.

5555 Darrow Rd.

Hudson, OH 44236

888-739-4120

www.joann.com

KATE'S PAPERIE

Beautiful papers, stationery, and accessories

72 Spring Street

New York, NY 10012

800–809–9880

www.katespaperie.com

K&COMPANY

Scrapbook papers and supplies. Use the store locator on their site to find retail stores that stock them.

www.kandcompany.com

MICHAELS

Scrapbook papers and supplies. There are many locations throughout the U.S.

8000 Bent Branch Dr.

Irving, TX 75063

800-642-4235

www.michaels.com

THE PAPER SOURCE

Handmade papers from all over the world. There are several locations throughout the U.S.

410 N. Milwaukee

Chicago, IL 60610

888-PAPER-11

www.paper-source.com

RANGER INDUSTRIES, INC.

Ink and craft supplies

15 Park Road

Tinton Falls, NJ 07724

732-389-3535

www.rangerink.com

XYRON

Adhesive applicator and supplies

800-793-3523

www.xyron.com

YASUTOMO AND COMPANY

Decorative papers, Japanese screw punch,
Mizuhiki paper cord, origami paper, and
double-sided tape

490 Eccles Avenue

South San Francisco, CA 94080

650-737-8888

www.yasutomo.com

Lighting

DAYLIGHT COMPANY

Color-correct lamps for the artist and crafter

866-DAYLIGHT

www.daylightcompany.com

OTT-LITE

Manufacturers of full-spectrum lighting

800-842-8848

www.ott-lite.com

Inspiration

If you are ever at a loss for words, you will
find the following quotations websites
very helpful with writing your greetings.

MOTIVATIONAL AND INSPIRATIONAL
QUOTES COLLECTION

www.inspirational-quotes.info

THE QUOTATIONS PAGE

This is a wonderful source for inspiring and
thought-provoking quotations from famous
people and literature.

www.quotationspage.com

Acknowledgments

I would like to thank my family, friends, and colleagues for their endless support and for encouraging me to create this book. I especially want to thank my dear friend and mentor Carol Duvall for making me look like I knew what I was doing while folding paper in front of the camera on *The Carol Duvall Show* and for being my head cheerleader in this project, as well as in life. Heartfelt thanks to my friends Kelly Erhlich, Donna Kato, and Suzanne Lamar for their unfailing support, optimism, and brilliant ideas.

I would like to thank the folks at GPC Papers for providing countless beautifully patterned papers to work with, and my employer, Yasutomo, for an endless supply of origami paper and a great place to work.

I would like to thank Melissa Bonventre at Random House/Potter Craft for her enthusiasm in getting this book underway, and Jennifer Graham for her direction and patience. Thank you to my dear friend and talented illustrator Pamela Grant for creating diagrams out of my scribbles and for checking the instructions. Thanks go out to Jack Deutsch for his beautiful photography and for making my stuff look good.

Most of all, a very sincere thank you goes out to the ladies and gentlemen who have attended my workshops and those who have been fans of my work over the years. I am grateful because without you, this book would not have been written.

Index

Published in the United States by Potter Craft,
an imprint of the Crown Publishing Group,
a division of Random House, Inc., New York.
www.crownpublishing.com
www.pottercraft.com

POTTER CRAFT and colophon is a registered trademark of
Random House, Inc.

Library of Congress Cataloging-in-Publication Data
Thomas, Karen Elaine.
Origami card craft : 30 clever cards and envelopes to fold
/ Karen Elaine Thomas.
     p. cm.
ISBN 978-0-307-40840-2
1. Origami. I. Title.
TT870.T518 2009
736'.982—dc22
2008019458

Printed in China

DESIGN BY DOMINIKA DMYTROWSKI
PHOTOGRAPHY BY JACK DEUTSCH
ILLUSTRATIONS BY PAMELA GRANT

10 9 8 7 6 5 4 3 2 1

First Edition